Houghton Mifflin
Math

North Carolina

 HOUGHTON MIFFLIN

BOSTON

Houghton Mifflin Math
North Carolina

Program Authors & Consultants

Authors

Dr. Carole Greenes

Professor of Mathematics Education

Boston University
Boston, MA

Dr. Matt Larson

Curriculum Specialist for Mathematics

Lincoln Public Schools
Lincoln, NE

Dr. Miriam A. Leiva

Distinguished Professor of Mathematics Emerita

University of
North Carolina
Charlotte, NC

Dr. Jean M. Shaw

Professor Emerita of Curriculum and Instruction

University of Mississippi
Oxford, MS

Dr. Lee Stiff

Professor of Mathematics Education

North Carolina State University
Raleigh, NC

Dr. Bruce R. Vogeli

Clifford Brewster Upton Professor of Mathematics

Teachers College, Columbia University
New York, NY

Dr. Karol Yeatts

Associate Professor

Barry University
Miami, FL

Consultants

Strategic Consultant

Dr. Liping Ma

Senior Scholar

Carnegie Foundation for the Advancement of Teaching
Palo Alto, CA

Language and Vocabulary Consultant

Dr. David Chard

Professor of Reading

University of Oregon
Eugene, OR

Grades K-3 Reviewers

Grade K

Hilda Kendrick
W E Wilson
Elementary School
Jefferson, IN

Debby Nagel
Assumption
Elementary School
Cincinnati, OH

Jen Payet
Lake Ave. Elementary School
Saratoga Springs, NY

Karen Sue Hinton
Washington Elementary School
Ponca City, OK

Grade 1

Karen Wood
Clay Elementary School
Clay, AL

Paula Rowland
Bixby North Elementary School
Bixby, OK

Stephanie McDaniel
B. Everett Jordan
Elementary School
Graham, NC

Juan Melgar
Lowrie Elementary School
Elgin, IL

Sharon O'Brien
Echo Mountain School
Phoenix, AZ

Grade 2

Sally Bales
Akron Elementary School
Akron, IN

Rose Marie Bruno
Mawbey Street Elementary
School
Woodbridge, NJ

Kiesha Doster
Berry Elementary School
Detroit, MI

Marci Galazkiewicz
North Elementary School
Waukegan, IL

Ana Gaspar
Lowrie Elementary School
Elgin, IL

Elana Heinoren
Beechfield Elementary School
Baltimore, MD

Kim Terry
Woodland Elementary School
West
Gages Lake, IL

Megan Burton
Valley Elementary School
Pelham, AL

Kristy Ford
Eisenhower Elementary School
Norman, OK

Grade 3

Jenny Chang
North Elementary School
Waukegan, IL

Patricia Heintz
Harry T. Stewart
Elementary School
Corona, NY

Shannon Hopper
White Lick Elementary School
Brownsburg, IN

Allison White
Kingsley Elementary School
Naperville, IL

Amy Simpson
Broadmoore Elementary School
Moore, OK

Across Grades

Jacqueline Lampley
Hewitt Elementary School
Trussville, AL

Rose Smith
Five Points Elementary School
Orrville, AL

North Carolina Teacher Advisory Panel Members

Stephanie McDaniel
Grade 1
B. Everett Elementary School
Graham, NC

Yvette Smith
Grade 1
Northeast Elementary School
Pikeville, NC

Jennifer Grogan
Grade 1
North Canton Elementary School
Canton, NC

Caroline Annas
Grade 2
Shepherd Elementary School
Moorsville, NC

Del Daniels
Grade 2
Meadow Lane Elementary School
Goldsboro, NC

Tracy McKeel
Grade 3
Rosewood Elementary School
Goldsboro, NC

Fran Coleman
Grade 3
Rosenwald Elementary School
Fairmont, NC

Janet Lee Blue
Grade 4
Rosenwald Elementary School
Fairmont, NC

Lynnetta Burton
Grade 4
Pleasant Grove Elementary School
Burlington, NC

Amy Janning
Grade 5
Rosewood Elementary School
Goldsboro, NC

Brenda Sharts
Elementary Director
Cleveland County Schools
Shelby, NC

Classification, Positions, and Patterns

STARTING THE UNIT

FINISHING THE UNIT

Algebraic Thinking Indicates lessons that include algebra instruction.   WR Indicates WEEKLY WR READER® Connection

v

UNIT 1 Classification, Positions, and Patterns

Getting Started With Numbers

STARTING THE UNIT

3 Comparing Sets, Data, and Graphing 43

4 Represent and Read Numbers 0–5 57

FINISHING THE UNIT

UNIT 2 Getting Started With Numbers

vi

Algebraic Thinking Indicates lessons that include algebra instruction.

Time and Money

STARTING THE UNIT

9 Time

10 Money

FINISHING THE UNIT

WR Indicates **WEEKLY WR READER® Connection**

Measurement

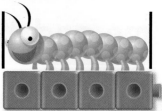

STARTING THE UNIT

FINISHING THE UNIT

Algebraic Thinking Indicates lessons that include algebra instruction.

UNIT 6 Measurement

Addition and Subtraction

STARTING THE UNIT

13 Addition

14 Subtraction

FINISHING THE UNIT

WR Indicates **WEEKLY WR READER® Connection**

Greater Numbers

STARTING THE UNIT

15 Numbers 10–20

16 Numbers Greater Than 20

FINISHING THE UNIT

BOOK RESOURCES

Algebraic Thinking Indicates lessons that include algebra instruction.   WR Indicates WEEKLY WR READER® Connection

UNIT 8 Greater Numbers

Name _____ Sot by Shape

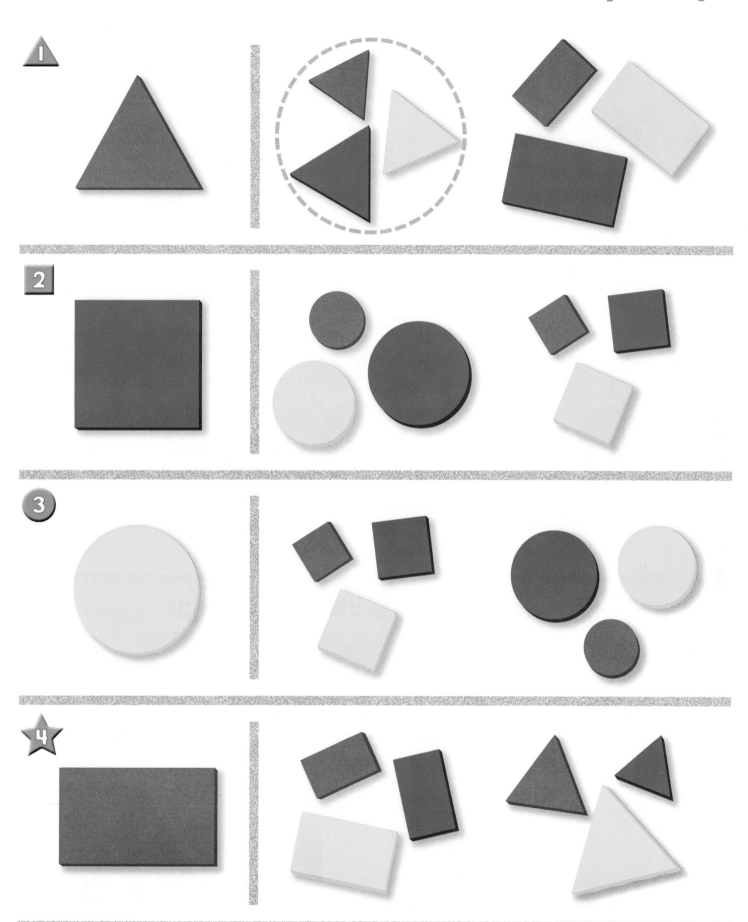

Directions 1–4 Circle the group where the shape belongs.

Problem Solving ▶ Visual Thinking

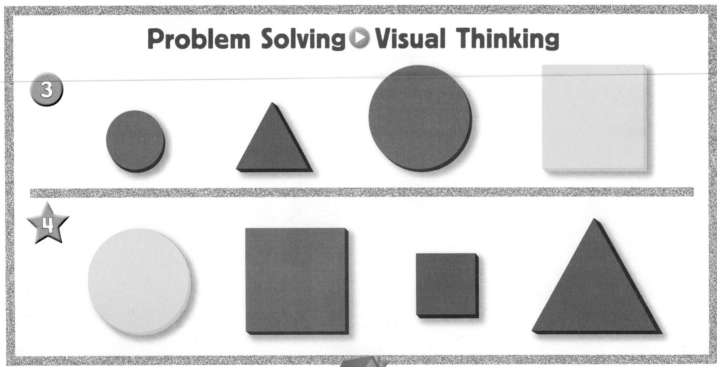

Directions 1-2 Circle the group where the shape belongs. 3 Circle the small red shape. 4 Circle the big blue shape.

At Home Collect 3 or 4 circular objects and 3 or 4 rectangular objects. Mix them up and have your child sort them by shape.

12

1

2

Directions 1 Circle the things that a person can wear. 2 Cross out the things that a person can eat.

Directions 1 Circle the things that a person can wear on the hands. 2 Cross out the things that a person can draw with.

At Home Give your child several grocery items such as cans, boxes, and bottles to sort by kind.

14

Name _____

Directions Cut out the pictures. Sort and glue them into two groups. Explain your sorting rule.

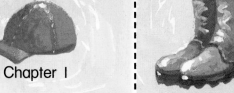

Chapter 1

15

Directions Cut out the pictures. Sort and glue them into two groups. Explain your sorting rule.

At Home Give your child 4 or 5 toys to sort into two groups. Have your child explain his or her sorting rule.

16

Name _____ Use Logical Reasoning

Directions Cross out the item that does not belong in a group of: 1 round things; 2 green things; 3 crayons; 4 small things. Explain your reasoning.

1

2

3

4

Directions Cross out the item that does not belong in a group of: **1** blocks; **2** thick brushes; **3** big things; **4** blue things. Explain your reasoning.

At Home Gather objects such as 3 spoons and 1 fork, or 3 crackers and 1 slice of bread. Have your child sort the objects by size, shape, or color.

18

Show and Tell

This take-home book will help you review concepts you learned in Chapter 1.

Color the caps to match each group.

Which shells are alike?

2

Where does this animal belong?

4

Where does my bead belong?

How can you sort these objects?
Tell your rule.

How are these objects alike?

6

Which one does not belong in my collection?
Tell why.

8

Name _____

Chapter Review / Test

Directions 1–4 Circle the group where the object belongs and tell why. **5** Cross out the one that does not belong and tell why.

eduplace.com/kids/mw/

Directions Sort the animals. Use a different color to circle each group. Name each group.

20

Name_____ **Inside, Outside**

Directions 1 Draw something red inside the bowl. Draw something blue outside the bowl.
2 Draw something orange inside the box. Draw something green outside the box.

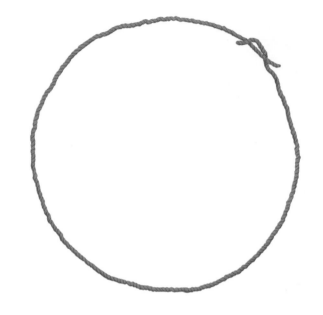

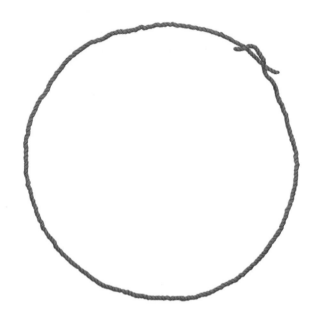

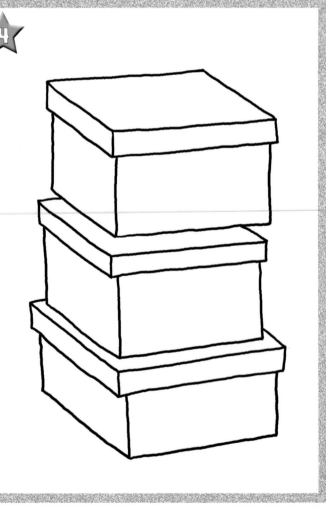

Directions | Draw a ball inside the circle. **2** Draw an X outside the circle. **3** Circle the child before the one in yellow. **4** Color the box that is on top.

At Home Have your child name items that are inside and outside drawers, cabinets, and other containers in your home.

Name _____ Extend Patterns

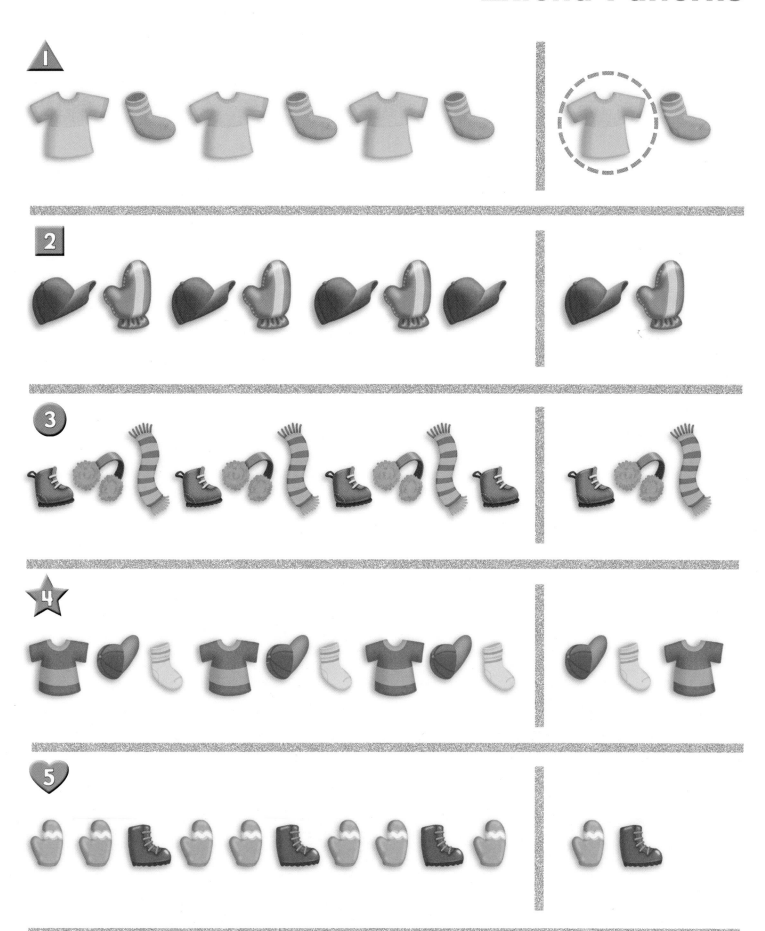

Directions 1–5 Circle the item that is likely to come next in the pattern.

Directions 1–5 Circle the item that is likely to come next in the pattern.

At Home Let your child use household items to make and extend a pattern, such as knife, fork, knife, fork, knife, fork.

Name _____

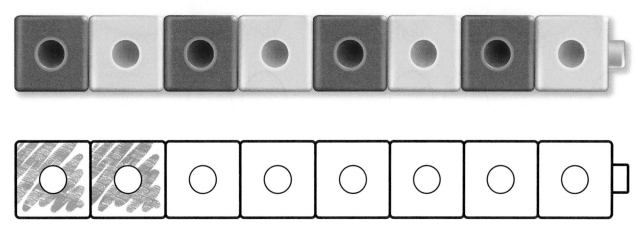

2

3

Directions 1–3 Find the pattern. Show the same pattern using different colors.

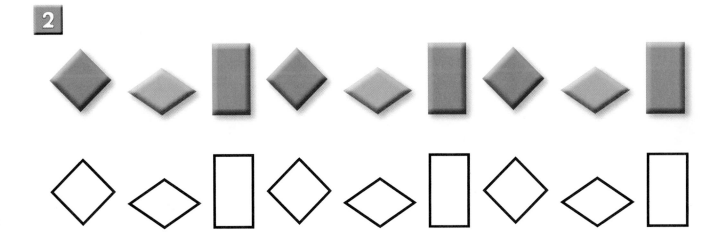

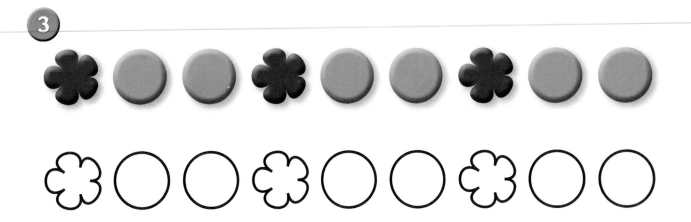

Directions 1–3 Find the pattern. Show the same pattern using different colors.

At Home Have your child tell how each pair of patterns shown above are alike and how they are different.

32

Name _____   **Use a Pattern**

Problem Solving

Directions Use pattern blocks to continue the pattern. Draw and color the blocks you used.

Chapter 2   **33**

Directions Use pattern blocks to continue the pattern. Draw and color the blocks you used.

At Home Have your child explain how each pattern in this lesson grows.

This take-home book will help you review concepts you learned in Chapter 2.

1

Which lunch box is before the blue one?

Which lunch box is in the middle?

2

What is inside the lunch box?

4

Color the grapes that are likely to come next.

Show the same pattern using different colors.

Draw the cracker that is likely to come next.

6

Tell how this pattern grows.

8

Name _____

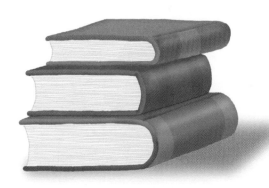

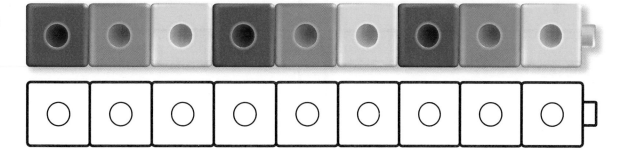

Directions Circle: **1** the bottom book; **2** the shoe outside the box; **3** the duck after the one in blue; **4** the sock that is likely to come next; **5** the dots that are likely to come next. **6** Show the same pattern using different colors.

NAME THE PATTERN

What You Need

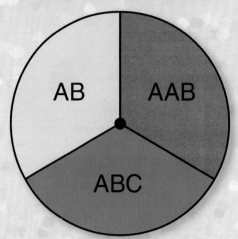

AB   AAB

ABC

How to Play | Take turns with a partner. **2** Spin the spinner. Place a counter on a space that shows that pattern. **3** Play until all the spaces are covered.

36

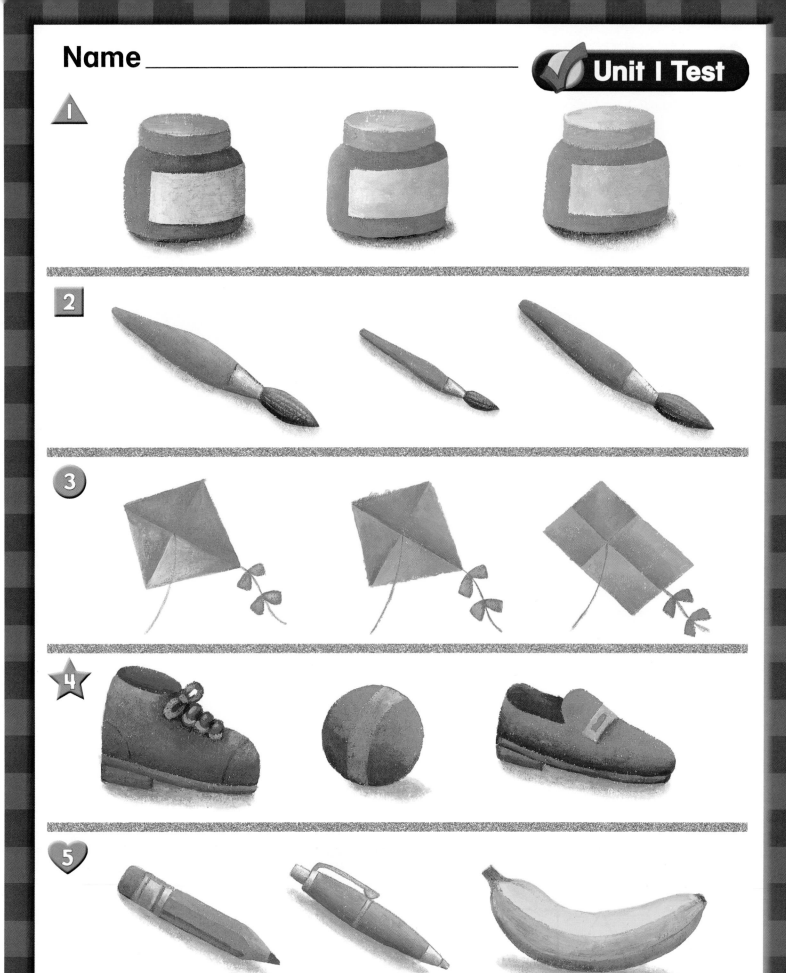

Directions Circle the objects that are the same: I color; 2 size; 3 shape; 4 kind. 5 Cross out the one that does not belong in a group of things to draw with.

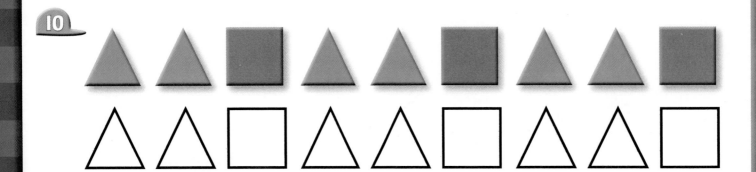

Directions 6 Circle the button in the middle. 7 Circle the animal between the ones in red.
8–9 Draw what is likely to come next. 10 Show the same pattern using different colors.

38

Sort by Two Attributes

Directions Place attribute blocks in the chart where they belong. Draw and color.

WEEKLY WR READER® Activity Almanac

See pages 321–324.

Name _____

1

2

3

4

5

Directions Circle: **1** the big shapes; **2** the group where the shape belongs; **3** the boy that is before the girl in green; **4–5** the shape that is likely to come next in the pattern.

Photography Credits: 5–6 © Ken Karp. 17–19 © Ken Karp. 38© Ken Karp. **Illustration Credits:** 2 © Don Stuart. 3–4 © Richard Garland. 7–8 © Peter Grosshauser. 13–14 © Peter Grosshauser. 15–16 © Richard Garland. 19(bml) © Peter Grosshauser. 19(bmr) © Nathan Jarvis. 19(b) © Peter Grosshauser. 20 © Richard Garland. Chapter 1 Story © Richard Garland. 21–22 © Nathan Jarvis. 23–24 © Don Stuart. 25–30 © Nathan Jarvis. 33–34 © Don Stuart. 35–36 © Nathan Jarvis. 37 © Don Stuart. 38 © Nathan Jarvis. 39 © Don Stuart. 40 © Nathan Jarvis. Chapter 2 Story © Don Stuart.

Use a Graph

Which do you like more?

Directions Ask four classmates which of these playgrounds they like more. Color a box for each response. Tell about your graph.

Which do you like the most?

Directions Ask four classmates which playground activity they like the most. Color a box for each response. Tell about your graph.

At Home Have your child explain the graph question and results. Ask your child to tell you what was chosen the most and the fewest.

54

What's in Ben's Sandbox?

This take-home book will help you review concepts you learned in Chapter 3.

I

Draw a pail for each child.

Draw lines to match one toy to each friend.

2

Are there more children or toys?

4

Are there fewer pails or shovels?

Look! Ben made a graph with his toys.
Does he have more trucks or tools?

How can Ben sort his toys?

6

Is there one toy for each friend?

8

Name _____

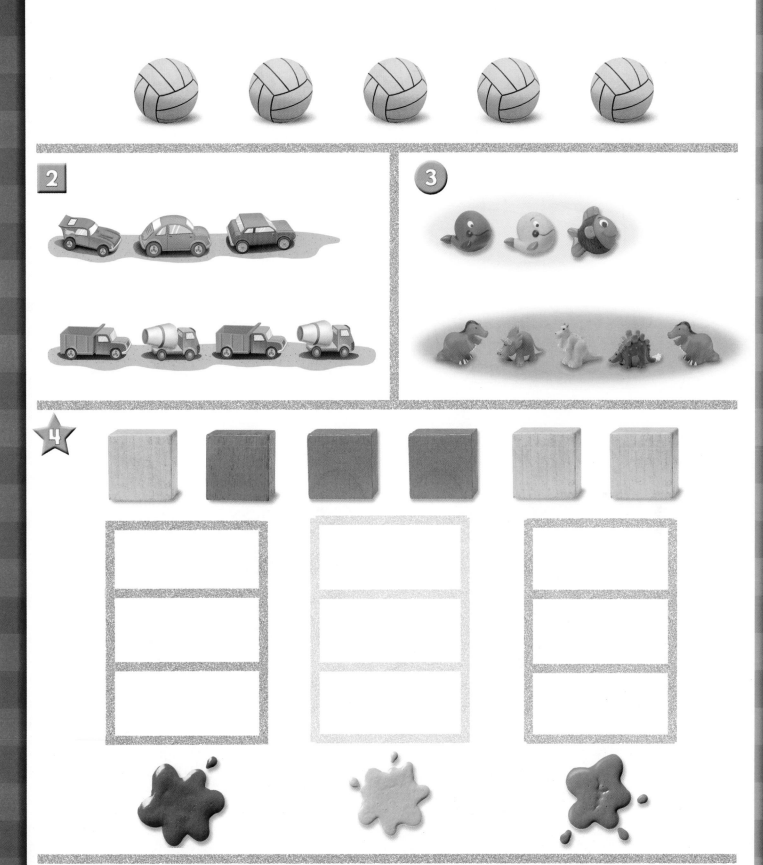

Directions 1 Draw balls to show the same number. 2 Circle the set with more. 3 Circle the set with fewer. 4 Draw blocks in the graph for each block in the picture. Circle the color with the most.

Directions Find two groups of living things in the picture. Count the number in each group. Compare the groups, using the words *more*, *fewer*, and *same*.

56

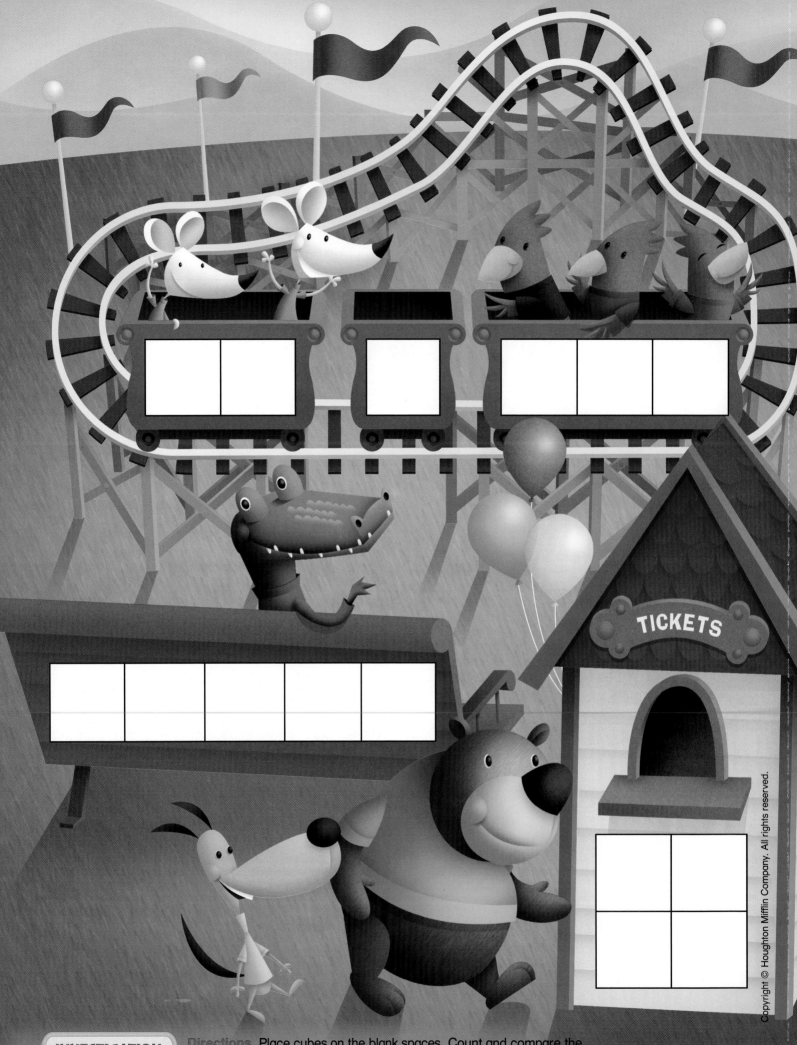

INVESTIGATION

Directions Place cubes on the blank spaces. Count and compare the numbers of cubes. Talk about other numbers of items in the picture.

One and Two

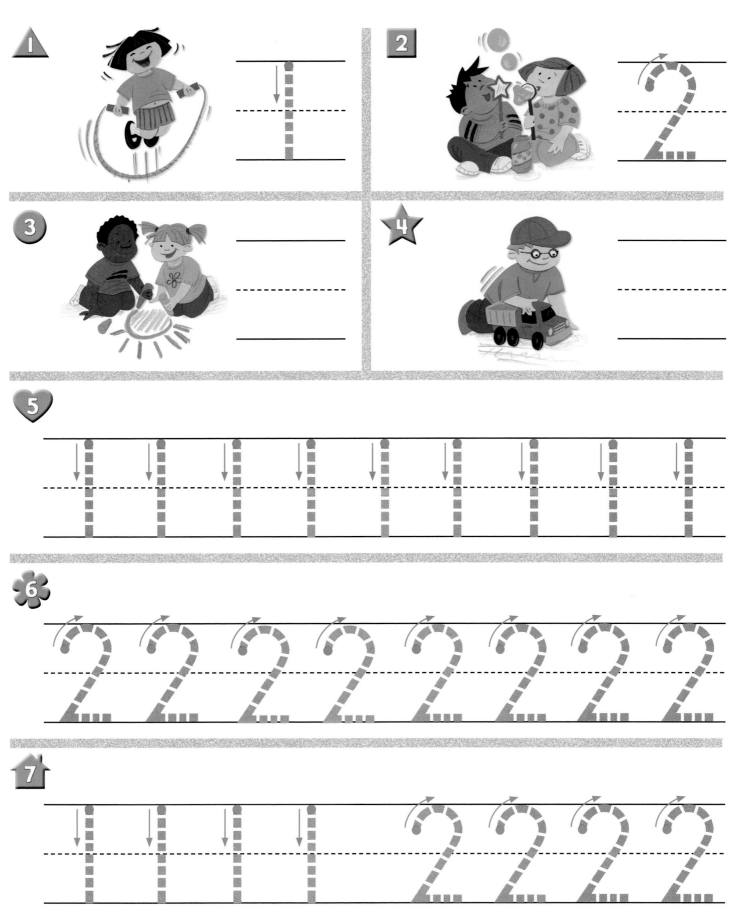

Directions 1–4 Count the children and write the number. 5–7 Write the numbers.

1

2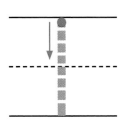

3

4

5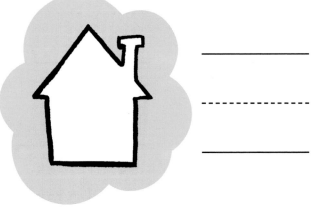

6

Directions 1–6 Count and color the shapes. Write the number.

At Home Have your child look around the room for examples of one and two items. Have your child practice writing the numbers 1 and 2.

Name _____ **Three**

 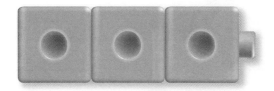

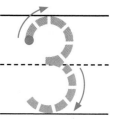

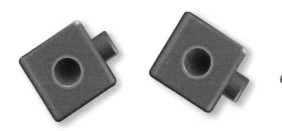

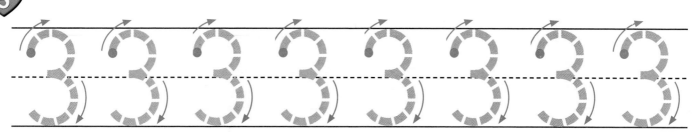

Directions 1–4 Place cubes on the pictures. Count and write the number. 5 Write the number.

1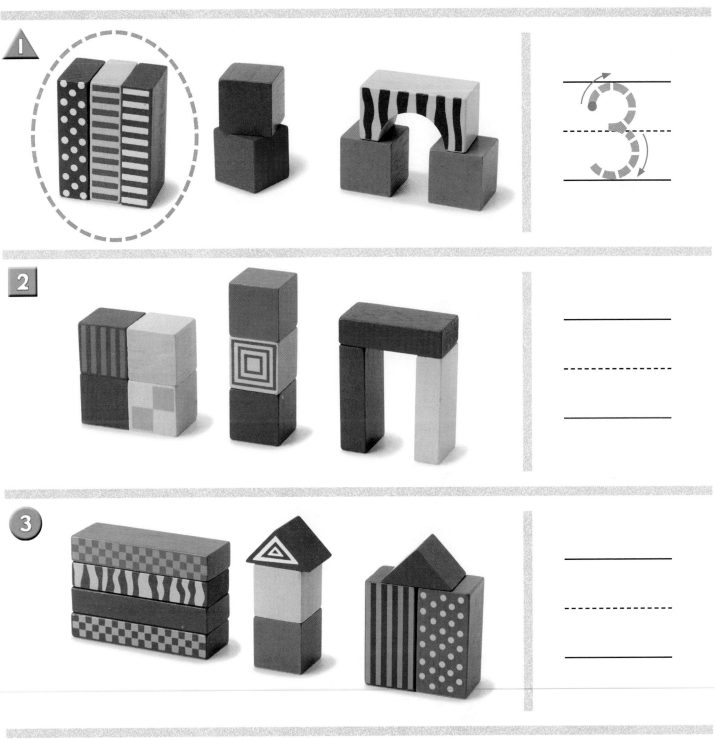

3

2

3

4

  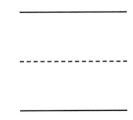

Directions 1–4 Circle the sets that show 3 blocks. Write the number 3.

At Home Have your child arrange 3 food cans in different ways and count the cans each time to see that there are 3. Have your child practice writing the number 3.

62

Name _____ **Four**

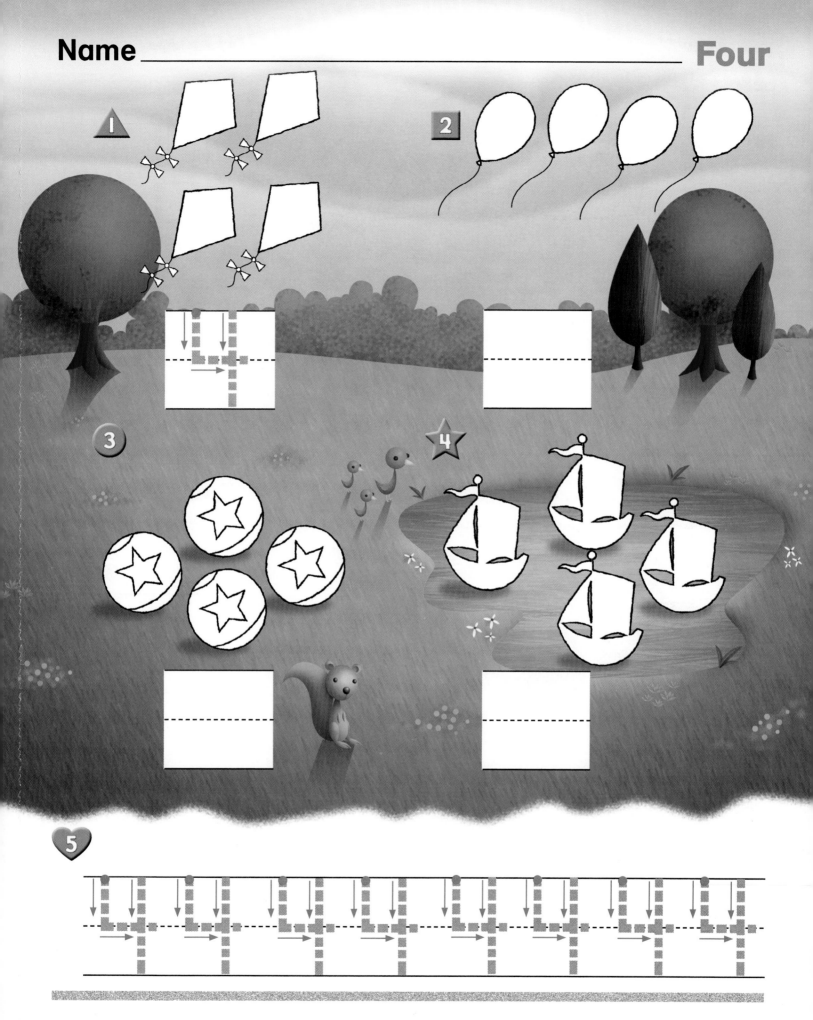

Directions 1–4 Count and color the items. Write the number. 5 Write the number.

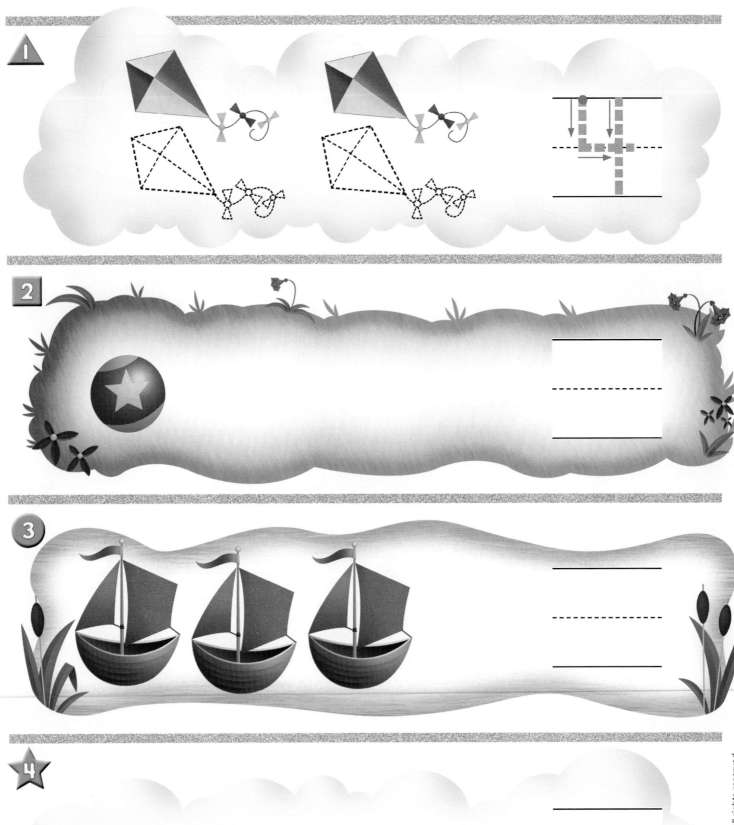

Directions 1–3 Draw more objects to show a set of 4. Write the number. 4 Draw a set of 4. Write the number.

At Home Have your child march as you count 1-2-3-4. Have your child practice writing the number 4.

64

1

2

5 5 5 5 5 5 5 5 5 5

Directions 1 Look at the groups of items. Circle the groups that show 5. 2 Write the number.

5

_____

- - - - - - - - - - -

_____

_____

- - - - - - - - - - -

_____

Directions 1-4 Count and color. Write the number.

At Home Have your child make sets of 5 items such as pennies, buttons, or paper clips. Have your child practice writing the number 5.

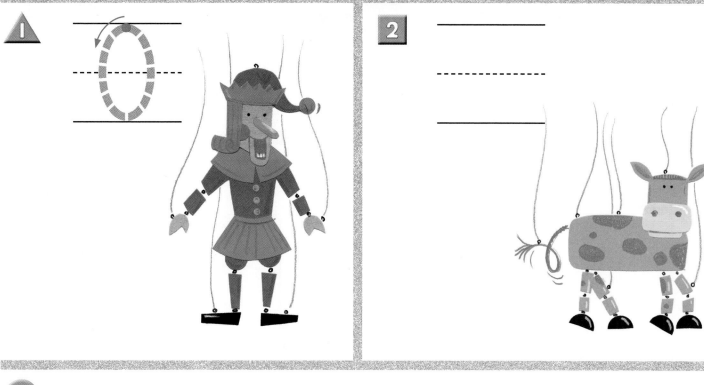

① 0

② ____

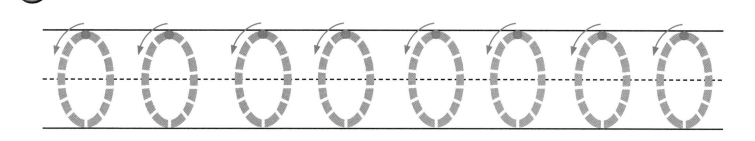

③

Directions 1–2 Look for the same puppet in the picture. Write the number to show how many you find. **3** Write the number.

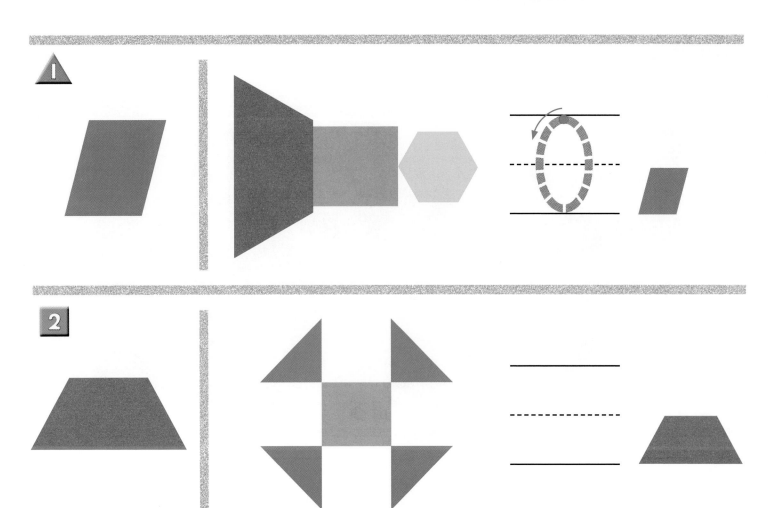

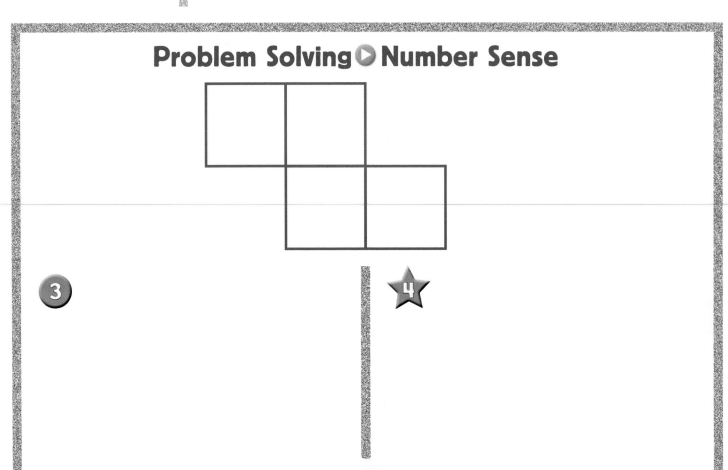

Problem Solving ▶ Number Sense

Directions 1–2 Look for the same block in the picture. Write the number to show how many you find. **3–4** Draw the same number of squares in a different way.

At Home Have your child tell you what zero means and what items you have zero of in your home. Have your child practice writing 0.

68

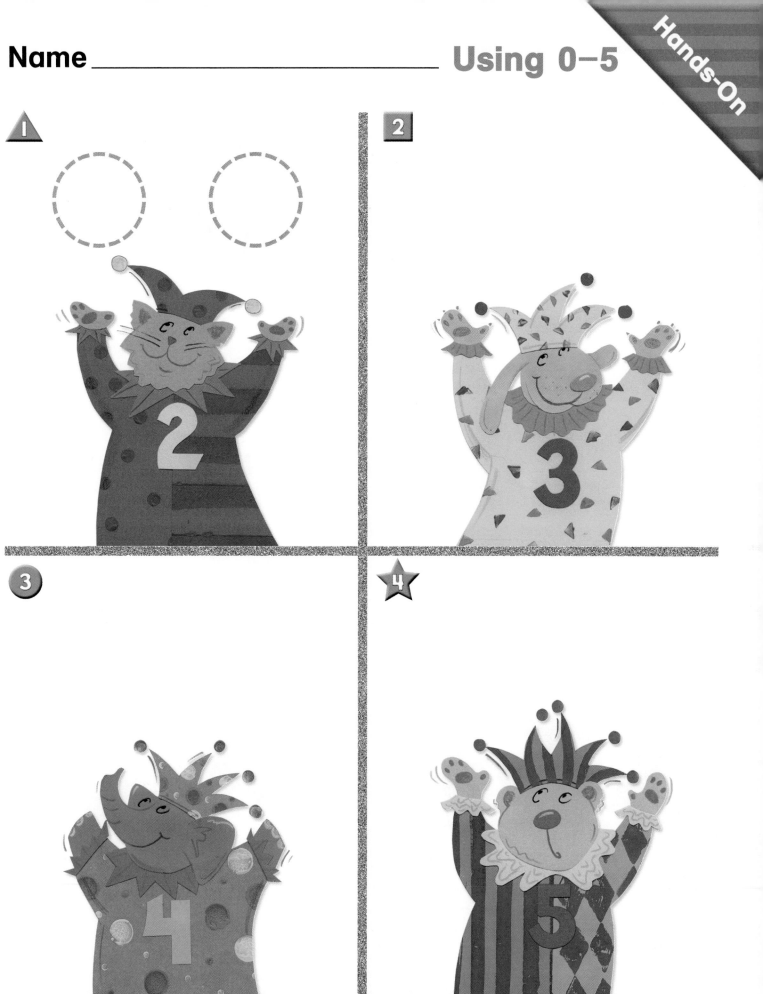

Directions 1–4 Use counters to show the number. Draw.

1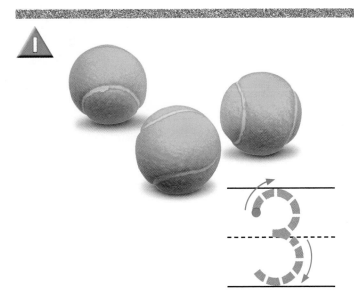

3

2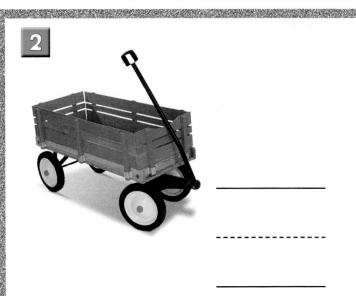

3

4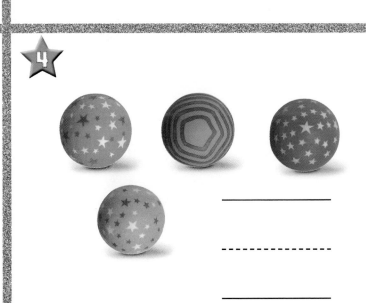

5

6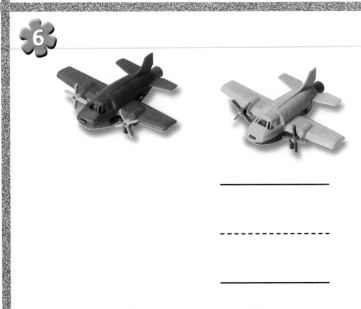

Directions 1–6 Count. Write the number of items in the set.

At Home Write a number from 0 to 5 and have your child show that number, using small items such as pennies or buttons.

70

Name _____

Use Logical Reasoning

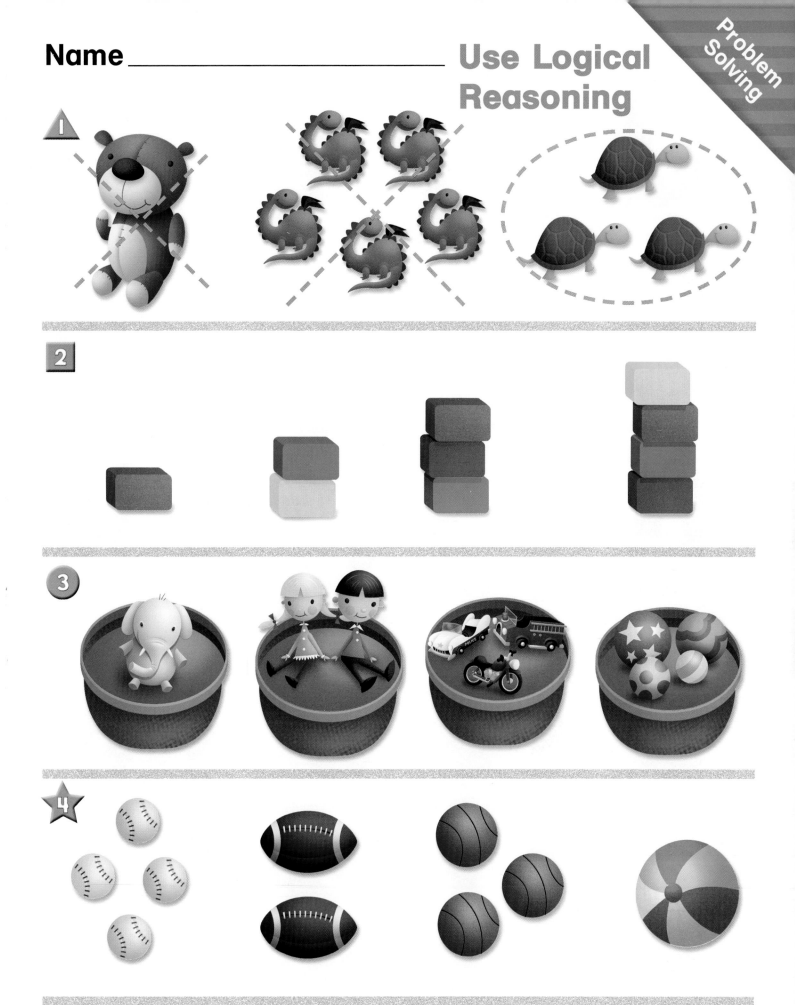

Directions 1–4 Listen to each clue. Cross out what does not match each clue. Circle what matches all the clues.

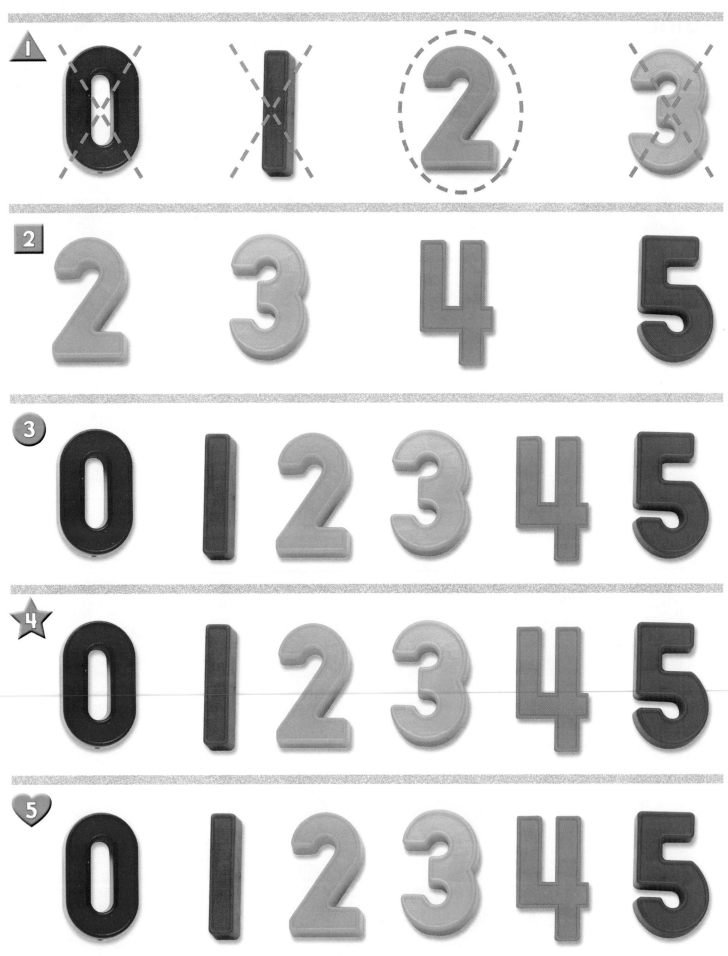

Directions 1–5 Listen to each clue. Cross out what does not match each clue. Circle what matches all the clues.

At Home Give your child two clues to guess a number from 0 to 5. For example: It is more than 3. It is fewer than 5. What is it?

Name _____

1

2

3

4

Directions 1 Circle the fourth bear. 2 Circle the third person. 3 Circle the fifth bug.
4 Circle the first person.

Directions 1 Circle the fifth person. 2 Circle the second bee. 3 Circle the first turtle. 4 Circle the fourth ant.

At Home Have your child line up five toys. Ask which is first? third? fifth? fourth? second?

All Dressed Up

This take-home book will help you review concepts you learned in Chapter 4.

1

How many hats does Tim have?

Let's see what Rosa and Tim find in this trunk.

2

How many gloves is Rosa wearing? _____

4

How many hats does Tim have now?

5

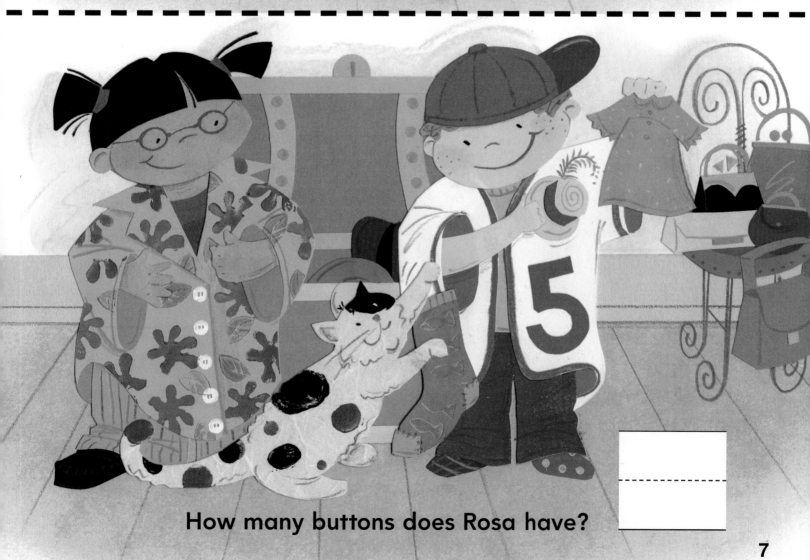

How many buttons does Rosa have?

7

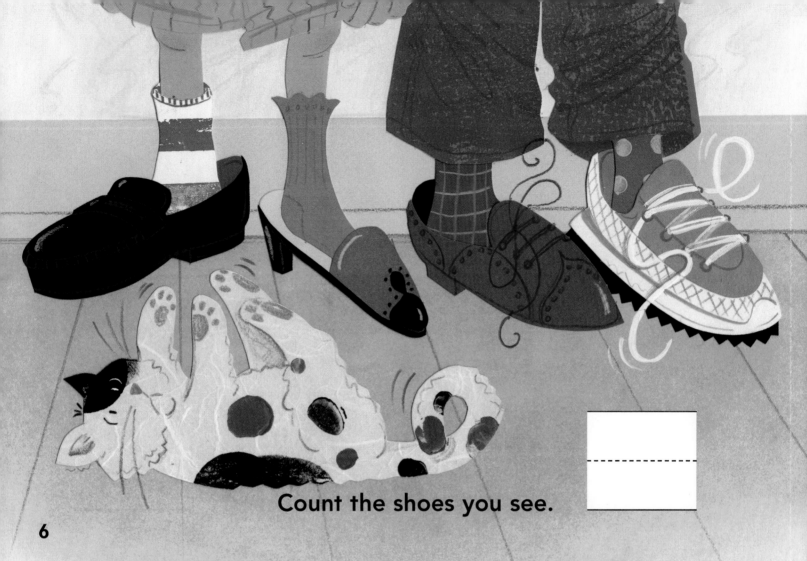

Count the shoes you see.

6

How many clothes are inside the trunk?

8

Name _____

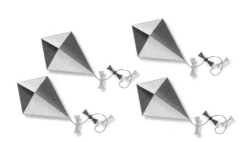  

_____
- - - - - - - - - - - -
_____

_____
- - - - - - - - - - - -
_____

Directions 1 Circle the group that shows 4. Write the number. 2 Circle the group that shows 2. Write the number. 3–4 Draw dots to show the number. 5 Circle the second turtle. 6 Circle the number that matches both clues. It is more than 3. It is not 5.

MATCH-UP

What You Need

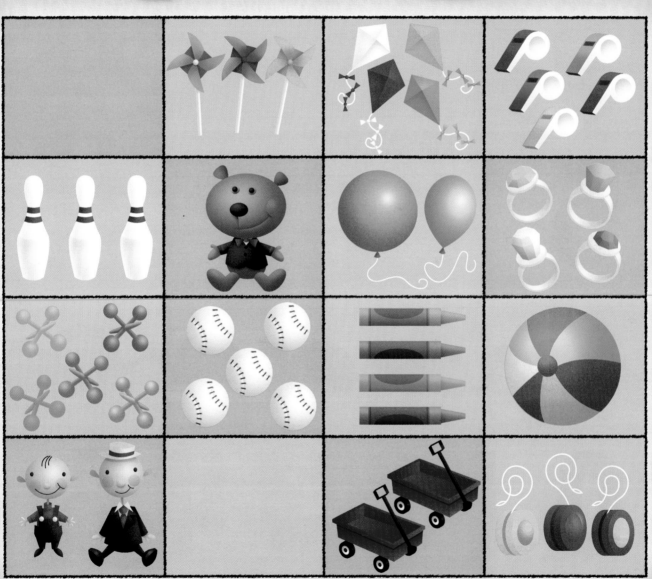

How to Play 1 Take turns with a partner. 2 Spin the spinner. Place a counter on a space that has that number of objects. 3 Play until all the spaces are covered.

Name _____

Unit 2 Test

Directions 1 Draw the same number of counters. 2 Circle the set with more. 3 Circle the set with fewer. 4 Circle the third carriage. Draw a line under the fifth carriage.

Unit 2

77

5
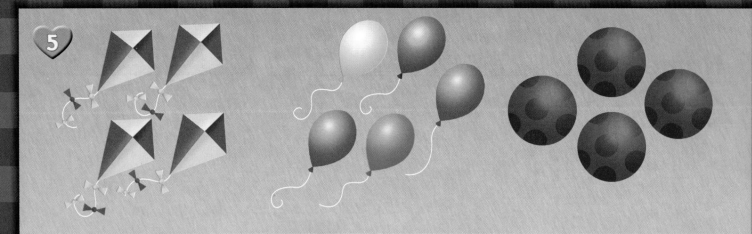

Which Has More?

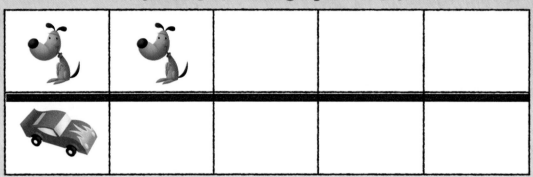

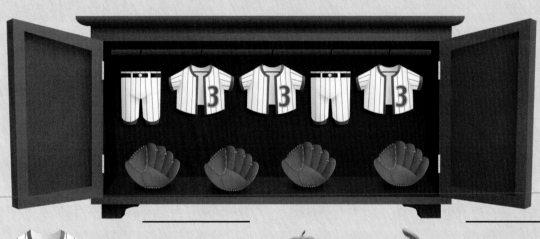

 7

_____
_____
_____

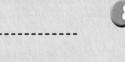 **8**

_____
_____
_____

 9

_____
_____
_____

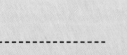 **10**

_____
_____
_____

Directions 5 Circle the set that shows 5. **6** Circle the row with more. **7–10** Look for each item in the picture. Write the number to show how many you find.

78

Name _____

Make a Table and Graph

Number of Toys

Toy	Number
(car)	_____
(airplane)	_____
(bear)	_____

Number of Toys

(car)			
(airplane)			
(bear)			

Directions Count the number of each kind of toy. Write the numbers in the table. Use the table to complete the graph. Tell about the graph.

Unit 2

WEEKLY WR READER® Activity Almanac

See page 325.

79

1

2

3

4

5 Favorite Toy

 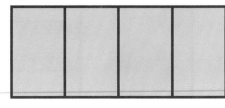

Directions I Circle the animal that is the same as the first one. Cross out the one that is different.
2 Circle the boat that is between the others. 3 Color to continue the pattern. 4 Match the items one to one.
Circle the set that has fewer. 5 Circle the favorite toy.

Photography Credits: 46(bm) © Ken Karp. 47 © Ken Karp. 48(t) © Ken Karp. 48(bl) © Radlund & Associates/Brand X Pictures/PictureQuest. 48(bmr) Corbis Images. 48(bml) © www.comstock.com. 48(br) © Corbis Images. 53(t) © Tony Freeman/PhotoEdit. 53(b) © Susan Van Etten/PhotoEdit. 54(t) © Mary Kate Denny/PhotoEdit. 54(m) © David Harrison/Index Stock Imagery. 54(b) © Jack Hollingsworth/Corbis. 55(t) © www.comstock.com. 55(mtr) © Ken Karp. 55(mbr) © Ken Karp. 62 © Ken Karp. 70(tl) © Radlund & Associates/Brand X Pictures/PictureQuest. 70(tr) © www.comstock.com. 70(b) © Ken Karp. 72 © Ken Karp. 75 © Ken Karp. 77(tm) © Ken Karp. 80(t) © Ken Karp. **Illustration Credits:** 42 © Chris Lensch. 43-44 © Dorothy Donohue. 47-48 © Dorothy Donohue. 49-50 © Ethan Long. 52-54 © Dorothy Donohue. 55 © Ethan Long. 56 © Bari Weissman. Chapter 3 Story © Dorothy Donohue. 57-58 © Chris Lensch. 59 © Liz Conrad. 60 © Ethan Long. 63-66 © Chris Lensch. 67 © Liz Conrad. 69 © Liz Conrad. 71 © Chris Lensch. 73-74 © Liz Conrad. 75(t) © Chris Lensch. 75(b) © Liz Conrad. 76 © Chris Lensch. 77 © Ethan Long. 78 © Chris Lensch. 79 © Liz Conrad. 80(t) © Richard Garland. 80(bl) © Chris Lensch. Chapter 4 Story © Liz Conrad.

Geometry, Fractions, and Probability

From the Read-Aloud Anthology

THE SHAPE OF THINGS

by Dayle Ann Dodds
illustrated by Julie Lacome

Access Prior Knowledge
This story will help you review
- Shapes

ISBN: 0-618-33873-X   Printed in the U.S.A.

MATH at Home

Dear Family,

We are starting a new unit called Geometry, Fractions, and Probability. In Chapter 5, we will identify plane shapes, equal parts, and symmetry. We will explore probability. In Chapter 6, we will learn about solid shapes.

Love, _____

Vocabulary

plane shape
A two-dimensional figure.

   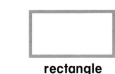

| circle | square | triangle | rectangle |

solid shape
A three-dimensional figure.

| sphere | cone | cube | rectangular prism | cylinder |

symmetry
When a figure can be divided in half so that it has two mirrored parts.

equal parts
When a whole object is divided into two or more parts that are the same size and shape.

  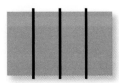

Vocabulary Activities

· Help your child find, describe, and identify plane and solid shapes in your home or neighborhood.

· Give your child a mirror to hold at the middle of a picture to explore mirror images and symmetry.

· Let your child help cut foods into equal parts such as halves.

 Technology
Visit *Education Place* at
eduplace.com/parents/mw/
for the Math Lingo Game,
e • Glossary, and more.

Literature to Read Together

● **Bear in a Square**
by Stella Blackstone
(*Barefoot Books, 1998*)

● **Shapes**
by Dr. Alvin Granowsky
(*Copper Beech, 2001*)

● **Eating Fractions**
by Bruce McMillan
(*Scholastic, 1991*)

Name _____   Equal Parts

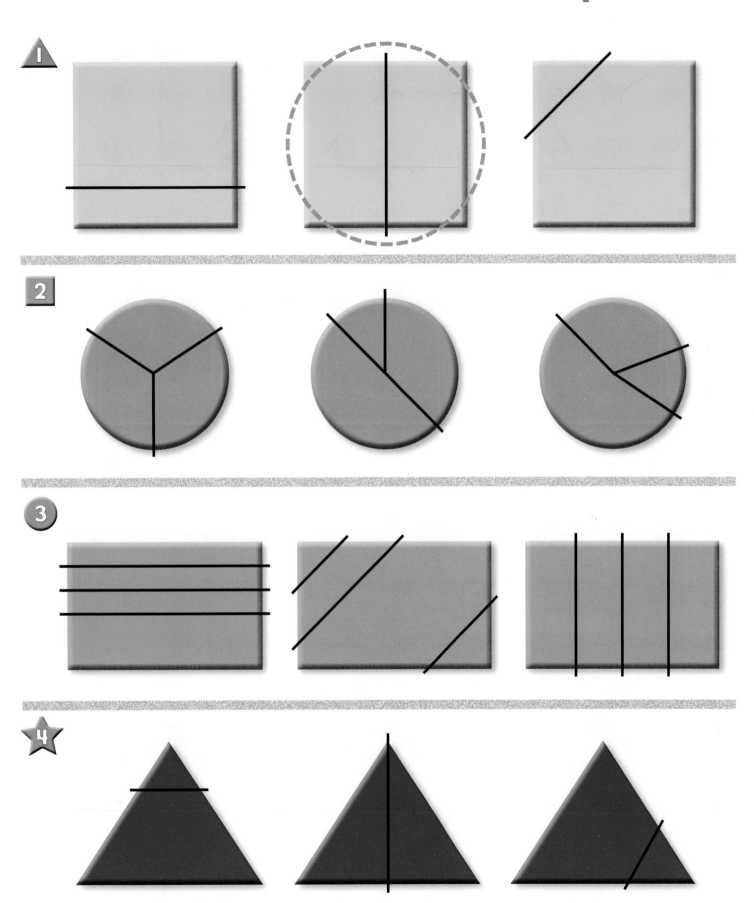

Directions 1–4 Circle the one that shows equal parts.

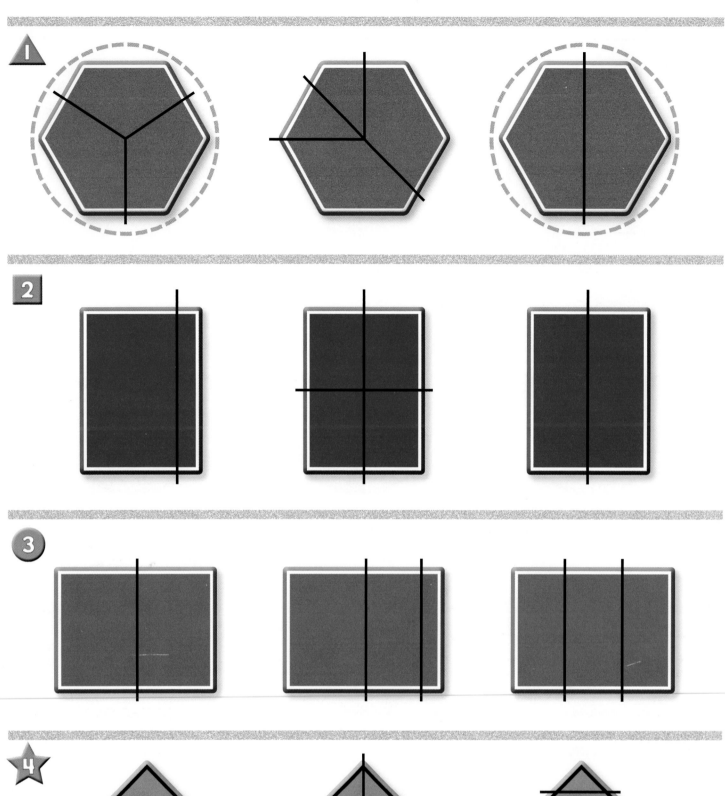

At Home Have your child find examples of items that are divided into parts, such as windows and sofa cushions. Have him or her tell whether or not the items show equal parts.

Name _____ **Halves**

Directions Circle the foods that show halves.

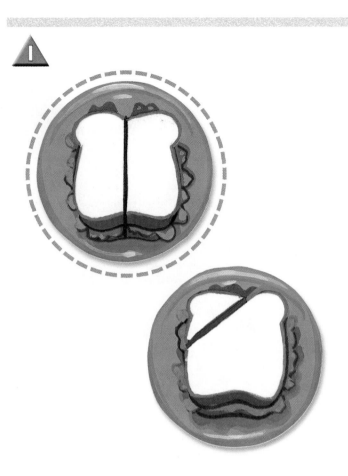

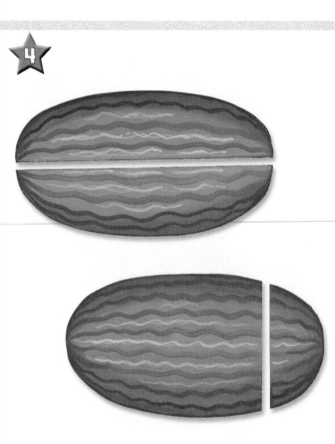

Directions 1–4 Circle the item that shows halves. Tell why the two parts are halves.

At Home Have your child explain which items in this lesson show halves and which don't. Discuss with your child foods that you might separate into halves.

1

2

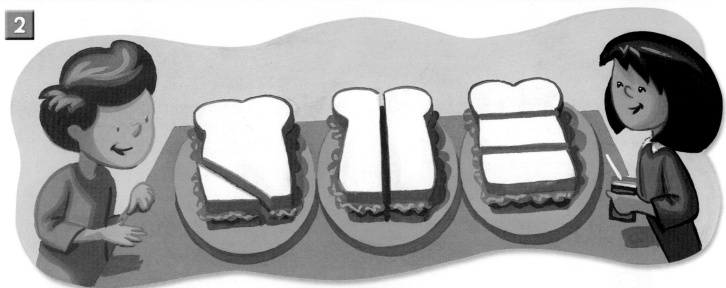

3

Directions 1–3 Count the number of children shown. Circle the plate of food that would give each child an equal part.

Directions 1–4 Count the number of children shown. Circle the plate of food that would give each child an equal part.

At Home Have your child help you cut and serve foods in equal parts for your family members.

Name_____

Predict and Record Outcomes

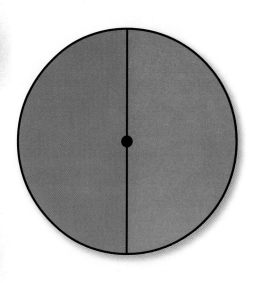

Spin and Tally

Color	Predict	Record
	_____	_____
	_____	_____
	_____	_____

Directions Predict how many times the spinner will land on each color if you spin five times.
Make a tally mark after each spin. Record the number of tally marks. Compare your predictions
to the outcomes.

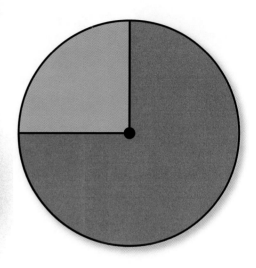

Spin and Tally

Color	Predict	Record
	_____ - - - - - - - - - - - - - - _____	_____ - - - - - - - - - - - - - - _____
	_____ - - - - - - - - - - - - - - _____	_____ - - - - - - - - - - - - - - _____
	_____ - - - - - - - - - - - - - - _____	_____ - - - - - - - - - - - - - - _____

Directions Predict how many times the spinner will land on each color if you spin five times. Spin and tally. Write the number of tallies. Compare to your predictions.

At Home Draw spinners like the ones in this lesson. Use a paper clip held by a pencil to spin. Have your child predict and record the outcomes.

I See Shapes!

This take-home book will help you review concepts you learned in Chapter 5.

1

I see rectangles.
How many do you see?

3

Shoes

BUS STOP

I see circles.
How many do you see?

2

I see squares.
How many do you see?

4

I see triangles.
How many do you see?

5

I see shapes with symmetry.
Which are the shapes with symmetry?

7

I see a shape pattern.
Draw the shapes that will likely come next.

6

I see shapes with equal parts.
Which shapes have equal parts?

8

Name _____

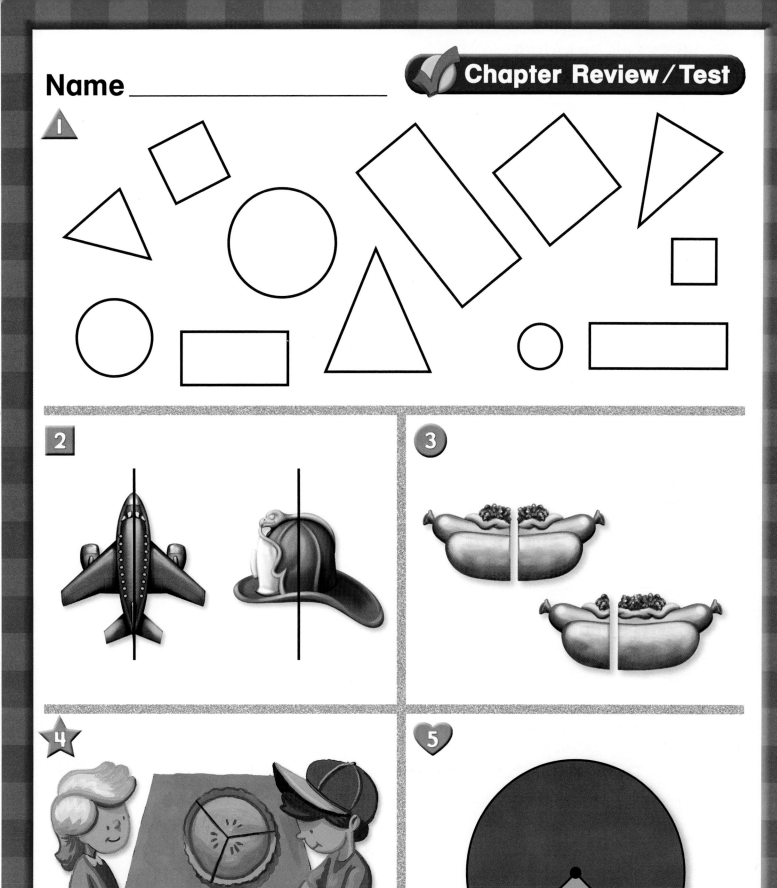

Directions 1 Color the rectangles blue, the triangles yellow, the circles green, and the squares red. 2 Circle the one with symmetry. 3 Circle the one that shows equal parts. 4 Circle the food that would give each child an equal part. 5 Put an X on the color you are more likely to spin.

Art
Connection

eduplace.com/kids/mw/

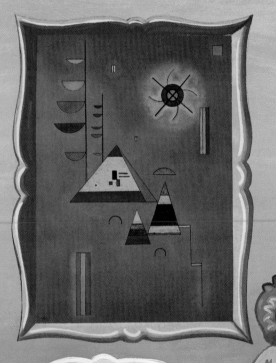

Directions Tell about the plane shapes you see in the paintings. Draw your own picture using at least two different shapes.

102

Make a Graph

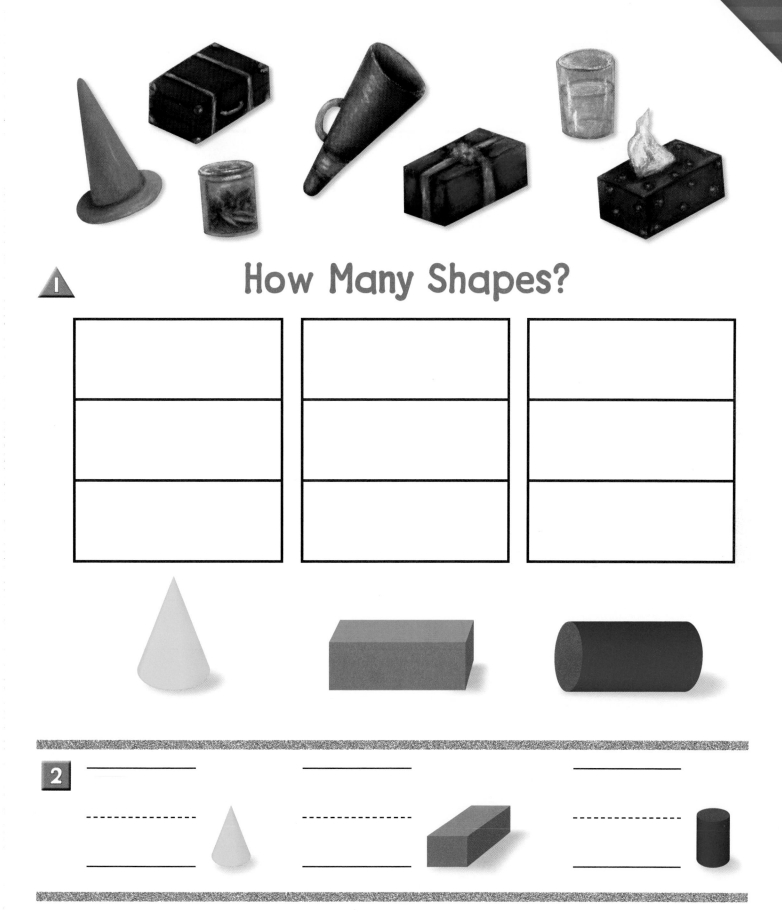

How Many Shapes?

Directions 1 Color one box in the graph for each item that is like the solid shape. 2 Count the colored boxes and write the numbers. Compare the numbers of shapes.

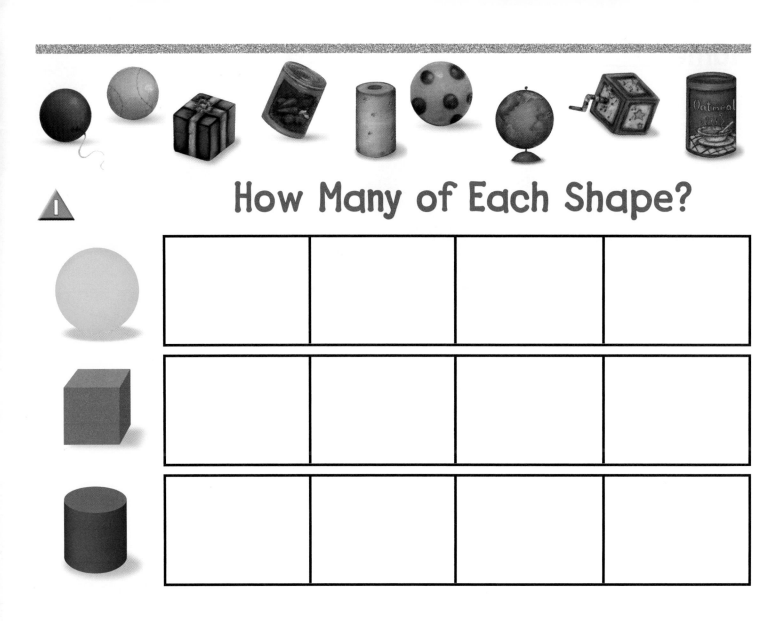

How Many of Each Shape?

△ 1

2

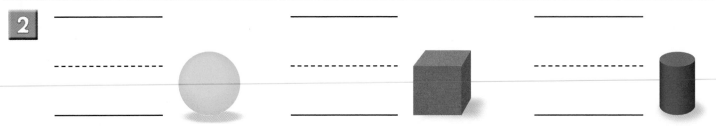

3

4

Directions 1 Color one box for each item like the solid shape. 2 Count the colored boxes. Write the numbers. 3 Circle the shape that has more. 4 Circle the shape that has fewer.

At Home Ask your child to tell you about the graphs and what they show.

114

A Shape Hunt With Patches

This take-home book will help you review concepts you learned in Chapter 6.

1

Find the ⬤ spheres.

3

Patches is on a shape hunt.
Help Patches find each shape.

2

Find the cubes.

4

Find the  rectangular prisms.

Which shapes can slide?
Which shapes can roll?

Find the  cones and the  cylinders.

6

Which solid shape made each shape print?

8

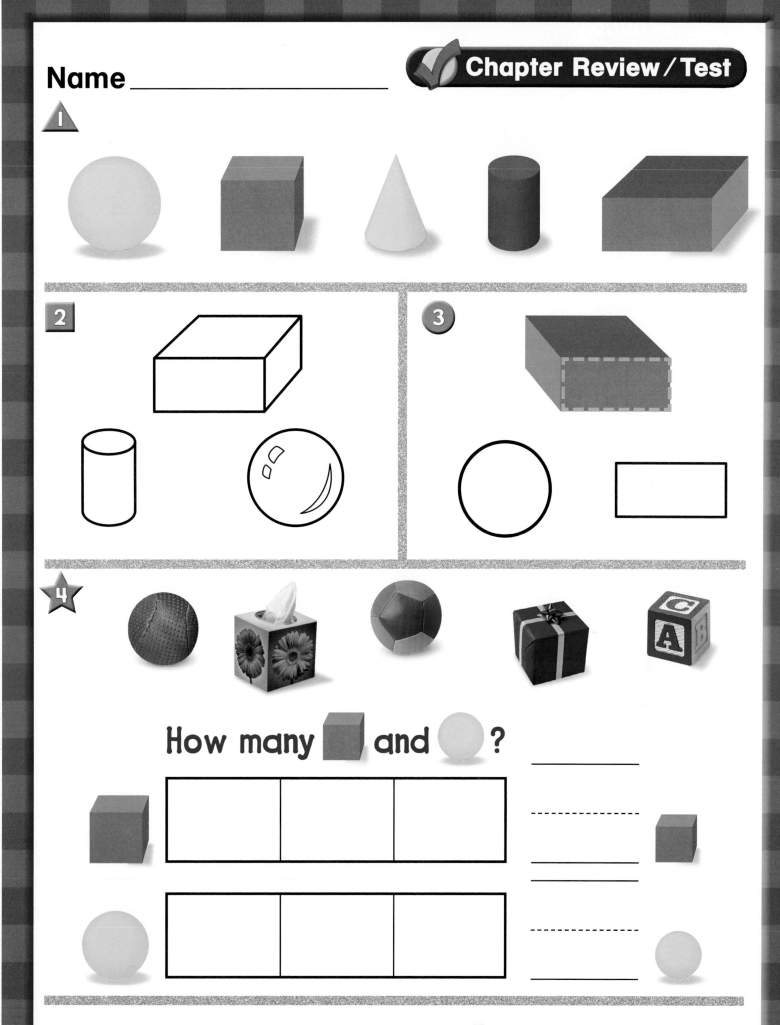

Directions 1 Circle the shapes that roll. 2 Color the sphere red, the cylinder yellow, and the rectangular prism blue. 3 Draw a line from the surface of the solid to the matching plane shape.
4 Color a box for each item that is like the solid shape. Write how many.

What You Need

SHAPE-O!

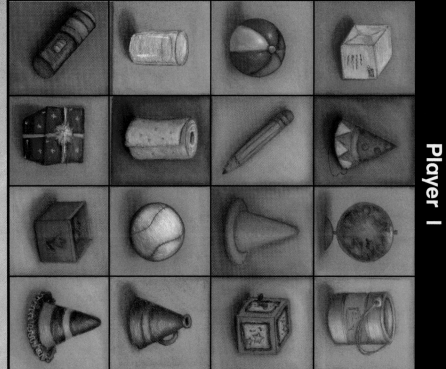

Player 1

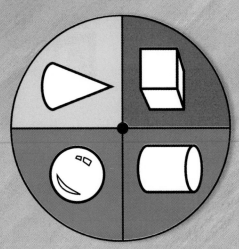

Player 2

How to Play **1** Take turns with a partner. **2** Spin the spinner and name the shape. Both players place a counter on a space that has that shape. **3** The first player to get 4 in a row calls out "Shape-O" and wins.

116

Name _____

1

2

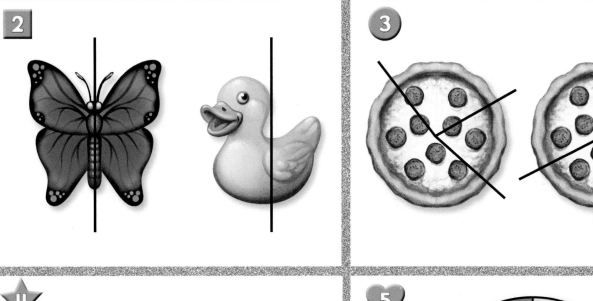

3

4

5

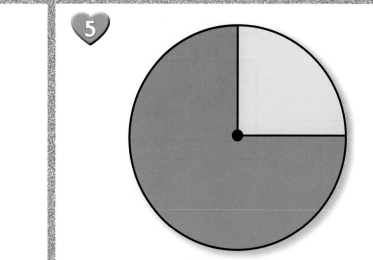

Directions 1 Color the circles red, the squares blue, the triangles green, and the rectangles yellow.
2 Circle the one with symmetry. 3 Circle the one that shows equal parts. 4 Draw a line from the surface of the solid to the matching plane shape. 5 Put an X on the color you are more likely to spin.

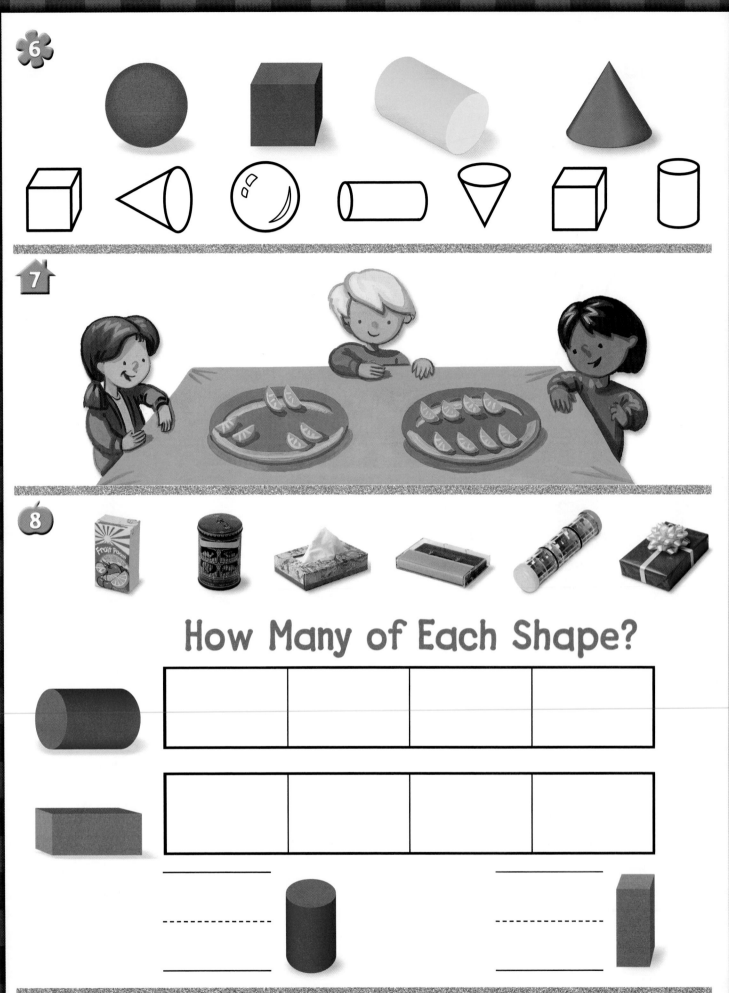

How Many of Each Shape?

Directions 6 Color the shapes to match the shapes at the top. 7 Circle the plate of food that would give each child an equal part. 8 Color a box for each item that is like the solid shape. Write how many.

118

Name _____

Paths and Mazes

1

2

3

4

Directions Start at the house each time. Follow the directions. Circle where you stop. **1** Go left 2 and up 1. **2** Go right 2 and down 1. **3** Go down 1 and left 3. **4** Go up 2 and right 3.

Unit 3

See page 326.

1

2

3

4

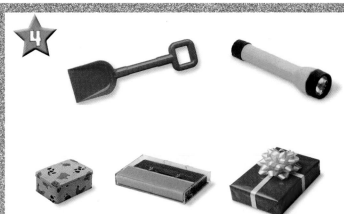

5

6

Directions 1 Circle the group where the shape belongs. 2 Circle the item that is likely to come next in the pattern. 3 Draw balls to show the same number. 4 Circle the set with more. 5 Color the triangles. Write the number. 6 Color the squares. Write the number.

Photography Credits: 102(bl) © 2005 Artists Rights Society (ARS), New York/ADAGP, Paris/Superstock. 102(tl) © 2005 Mondrian/Holtzman Trust/Artists Rights Society (ARS), New York/Giraudon/Art Resource, NY. 102(tr) © 2005 Artists Rights Society (ARS), New York/VG Bild-Kunst, Bonn/Giraudon/Art Resource. 107(1tl); 107(2trm); 107(2bl); 107(4bl); 108(3tr); 108(4tr); 110(br); 115(rm); 118(r); 120(1l); 120(3l); 120(3ml); 120(3r); 120(4br) © C Squared Studios/PhotoDisc/Getty Images. 107(3tr) © Stockbyte/ PictureQuest. 107(3br); 108(2bm); 108(3br) © www.comstock.com. 108(2tr) © Burke/Triolo/Brand X Pictures/PictureQuest. 108(3bm); 108(4tl); 110(bl) © Corbis Images. 108(4tm) © Siede Preis/PhotoDisc/Getty Images. 108(4bm) © Radlund & Associates/Brand X Pictures/PictureQuest. 120(4tl) © Stockbyte/ Picturequest. All remaining photographs © Ken Karp.
Illustration Credits: 82-84; 95-98; 101(bl); 102; 118 © Kenneth Spengler. 91-92; 101(ml); 101(mr); 117; 119; Mark and Rosemary Jarman. 99-100; Chapter 5 Story © Benrei Haung. 103-106; 113-114; 116 © Marisol Sarrazin. 111-112 © Patrick Gnan. Chapter 6 Story © Wayne Parmenter.

Numbers Through 12

From the Read-Aloud Anthology

James AND THE Rain

by Karla Kuskin

illustrated by Reg Cartwright

Access Prior Knowledge

This story will help you review

- Counting to 5
- Comparing Groups

ISBN: 0-618-33874-8   Printed in the U.S.A.

MATH at Home

Dear Family,

We are starting a new unit called *Numbers Through 12*. In Chapter 7, we will count, read, and write numbers 6 through 12. In Chapter 8, we will name, order, and compare numbers through 12. We will also estimate numbers of objects in a group.

Love, _____

Vocabulary

number pattern
A sequence of numbers arranged according to some rule.

12, 11, 10, 9, 8, 7, 6
backward by ones

2, 4, 6, 8, 10, 12
forward by twos

more, fewer
Words used to compare numbers of objects.

There are more frogs than ducks.
There are fewer ducks than frogs.

greater than, less than
Words used to compare numbers.

7 is greater than 5.
5 is less than 7.

Vocabulary Activities

• Help your child look for numbers on grocery items and buildings.

• Write a sequence of numbers leaving out one number. Have your child find the missing number.

• Give your child two groups of items. Have your child tell which group has more and which has fewer.

 **Technology**

Visit *Education Place* at **eduplace.com/parents/mw/** for the Math Lingo Game, *e* • Glossary, and more.

Literature to Read Together

● **Feast for 10**
by Cathryn Falwell
(Clarion Books, 1993)

● **Anno's Counting Book**
by Mitsumasa Anno
(HarperCollins, 1977)

● **Little Rabbits' First Number Book**
by Alan Baker
(Kingfisher, 1998)

Represent and Read
Numbers 6–12

INVESTIGATION

Directions Count and compare the numbers of animals in each group. Circle the group that has five. Use counters to show a group with one more. Draw the group.

124

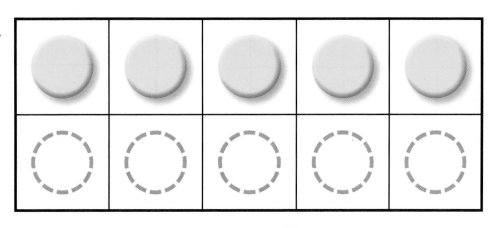

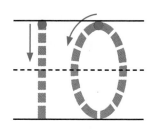

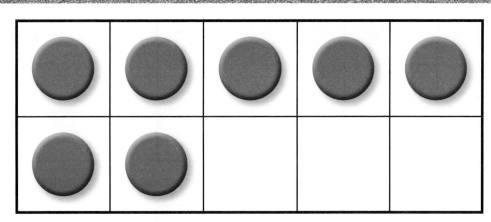

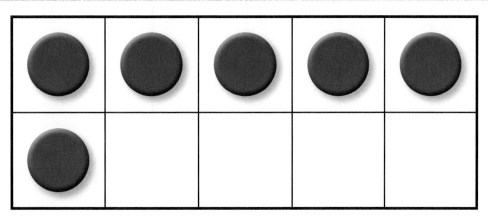

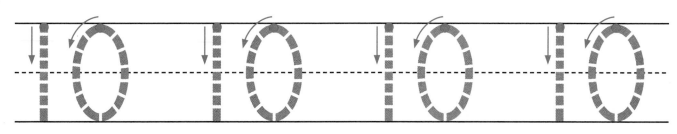

Directions 1–3 Place counters in the ten-frame to make 10. Draw. Write the number.
4 Write the number.

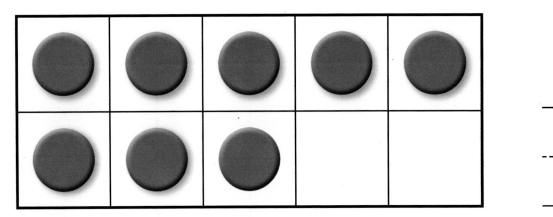

_____

- - - - - - - - - - - - -

_____

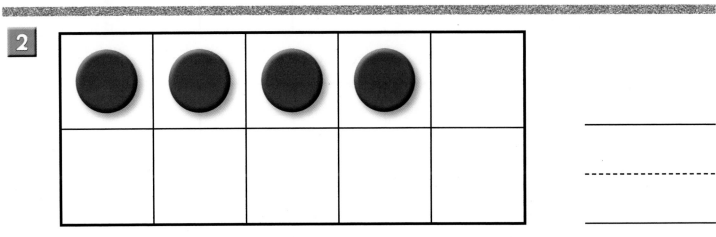

_____

- - - - - - - - - - - - -

_____

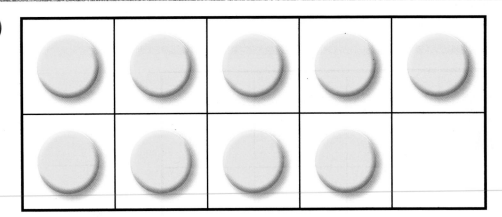

_____

- - - - - - - - - - - - -

_____

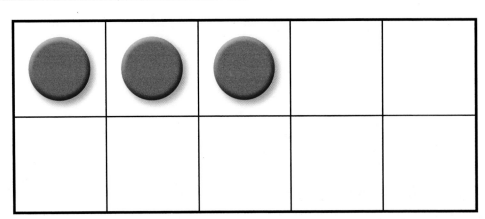

_____

- - - - - - - - - - - - -

_____

Directions 1–4 Place counters in the ten-frame to make 10. Draw. Write the number.

At Home Have your child point to and count the circles in each ten-frame. Have your child draw 10 objects and practice writing the number 10.

134

Problem Solving

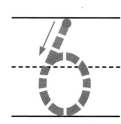

1   2   3   4   5   6

2

7   6   5   4   3   ___

3

1   3   5   ___   9

Directions 1–3 Count the items. Look for a pattern. Write the missing number.

5   6   7   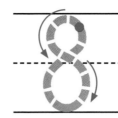   9   10

2

3   4   5   6   _____   _____

3

10   9   8   7   _____   _____

4

9   8   _____   6   5   _____

5

2   4   _____   8   _____   12

Directions 1–5 Look for a pattern in the numbers.
Write the missing numbers.

At Home Have your child read the numbers and
explain the patterns in each exercise. Start a
number pattern and have your child tell you the
number that comes next.

 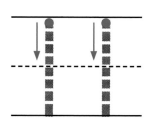

2

3

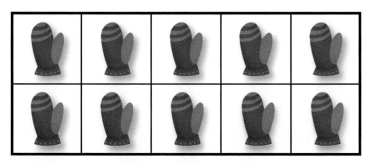

4

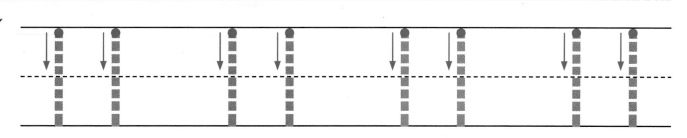

Directions 1–3 Count the items. Write the number. 4 Write the number.

1

9

10

(11)

2

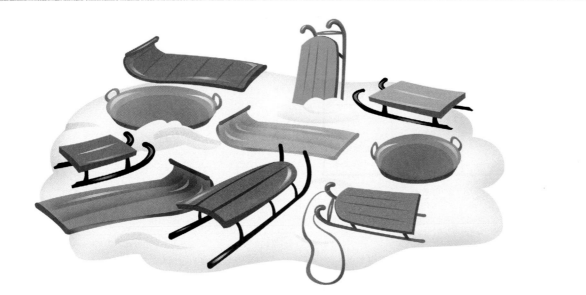

9

10

11

3

9 10 11

4

9 10 11

Directions 1–4 Count the items. Circle the number.

At Home Have your child point out the groups of 11 on this page. Listen as your child points to and counts the items one by one.

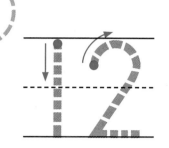

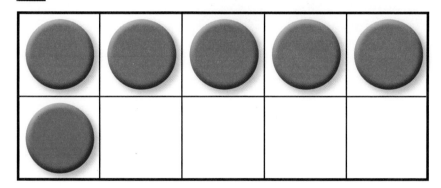

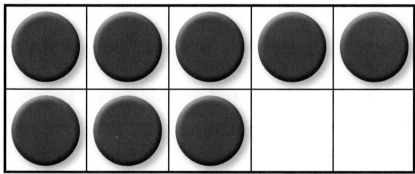

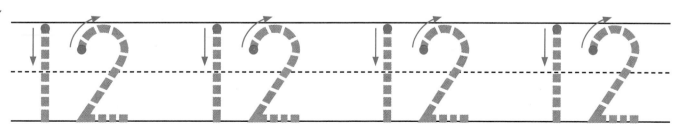

Directions 1–3 Use counters to make 12. Draw the counters. Write the number.
4 Write the number.

_____

- - - - - - - - - - - -

_____

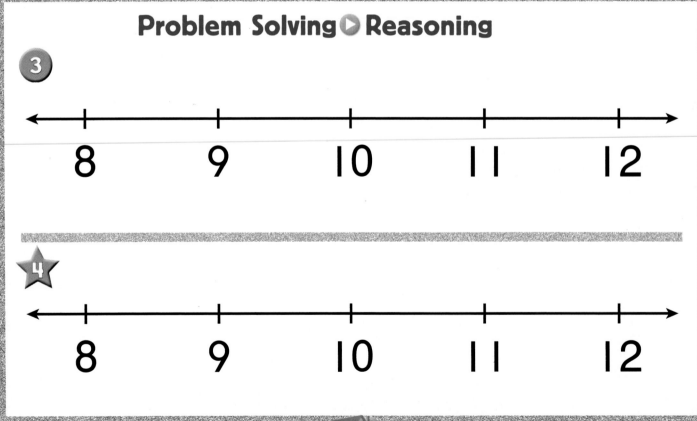

_____

- - - - - - - - - - - -

_____

Problem Solving ▶ Reasoning

③

8   9   10   11   12

④

8   9   10   11   12

Directions 1–2 Count the items. Draw more to make 12. Write the number. **3–4** Listen to each clue. Cross out what does not match each clue. Circle what matches all the clues.

At Home Let your child count a dozen eggs, 12 pieces of silverware, and 12 pennies. Have your child show you how to write 12.

140

FOLLOW THE TRACKS

This take-home book will help you review concepts you learned in Chapter 7.

Follow the tracks to the grass.
How many tracks do you see?

Follow the tracks to the tree.
How many tracks do you see?

2

Follow the tracks to the berries.
How many tracks do you see?

4

Follow the tracks to the carrot.
How many tracks do you see?

Follow the tracks to the corn.
How many tracks do you see?

Follow the tracks to the acorns.
How many tracks do you see?

6

Follow the tracks to the seeds.
Draw more tracks to make 12.

8

Name _____

_____

- - - - - - - - - - - - -

_____

_____

- - - - - - - - - - - - -

_____

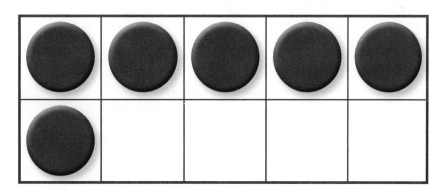

_____

- - - - - - - - - - - - -

_____

10

11

12

_____   _____

- - - - - - -   - - - - - - -

12 11 10 _____ _____ 7

Directions 1 Circle the group that shows 7. Write the number. 2 Circle the group that shows 9. Write the number. 3 Place counters in the ten-frame to make 10. Draw. Write the number. 4 Count the trees. Circle the number. 5 Look for a pattern. Write the missing numbers.

Chapter 7

141

November

Sunday	Monday	Tuesday	Wednesday	Thursday	Friday	Saturday
	1	2	3	4	5	6
7	8	9	10	11	12	13
14	15	16	17	18	19	20
21	22	23	24	25	26	27
28	29	30				

1.  _____

2.  _____

3.  _____

4.  _____

Directions 1–4 Look for the weather symbol on the calendar. Count. Write the number you find.

Using Numbers 0-12

8

7

6

9

INVESTIGATION **Directions** Draw more kites to show each number. Talk about the number of kites shown and the number of kites you drew in each picture.

144

Name _____

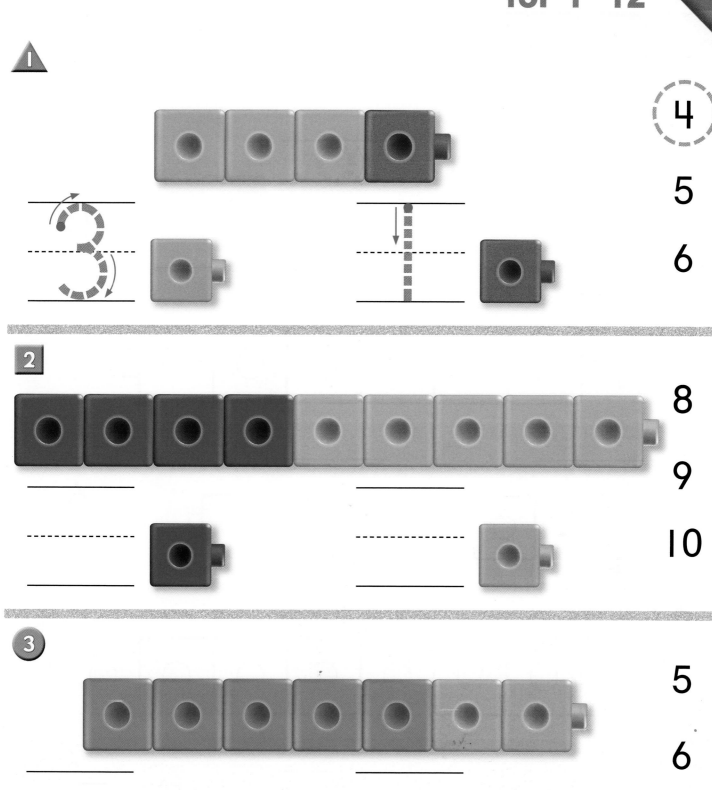

1

3

4
5
6

2

8
9
10

3

5
6
7

Directions 1–3 Build the cube train. Count the cubes. Circle the number.
Count the cubes of each color. Write the numbers.

▲ 1

2   8

10
11
12

2

_____
- - - - - - - -

_____
- - - - - - - -

5
6
7

3

_____
- - - - - - - -

_____
- - - - - - - -

7
8
9

Directions 1–3 Count the cubes. Circle the number.
Color some cubes one color and the rest another color.
Write the number of each color.

At Home Have your child divide 12 pennies into
2 groups and tell how many are in each group. For
example, 11 and 1, 10 and 2, 9 and 3, 8 and 4, 7
and 5, 6 and 6.

Order Numbers to 12

1

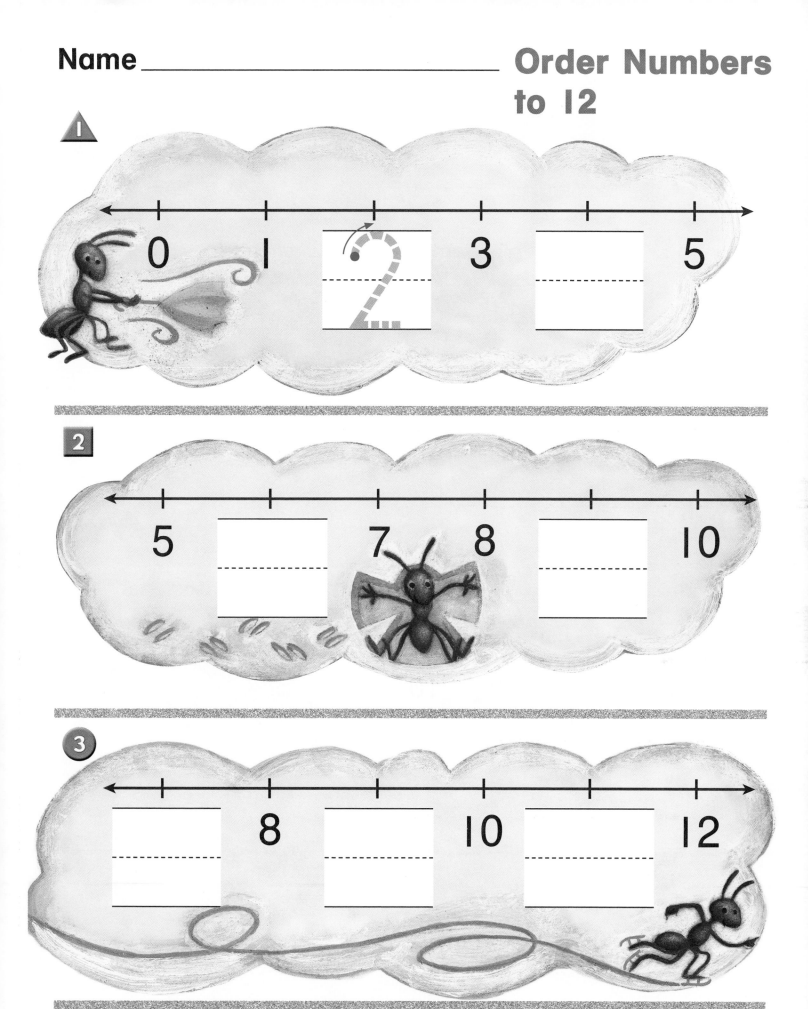

0   1   2   3   ___   5

2

5   ___   7   8   ___   10

3

___   8   ___   10   ___   12

Directions 1–3 Write the missing numbers.

Directions Connect the dots. Color the picture.

At Home Help your child write the numbers 1 through 12 on small pieces of paper, mix them up, and put them in order.

Sort by Number

Directions Circle sets of 7 with red. Circle sets of 10 with blue.

1

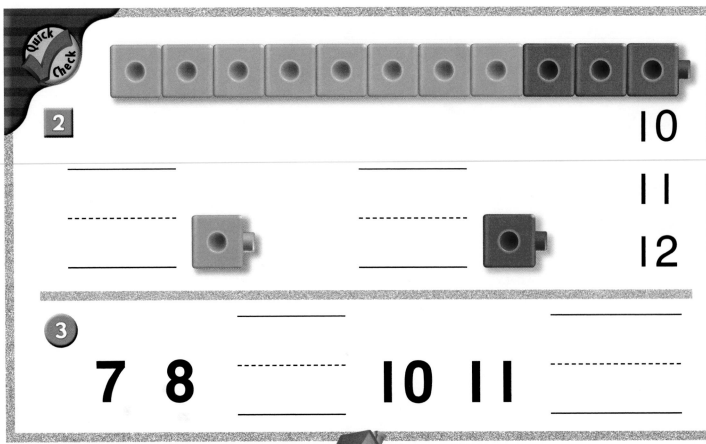

2

10

11

12

3

7   8   ___   10   11   ___

Directions 1 Circle sets of 4 with red. Circle sets of 6 with blue. 2 Build the cube train. Circle the number. Count the cubes of each color. Write the numbers. 3 Write the missing numbers.

At Home Using small items such as buttons, make two sets of 5 and two sets of 7. Have your child count each set and tell which sets have the same number.

150

Name_____ **More and Fewer**

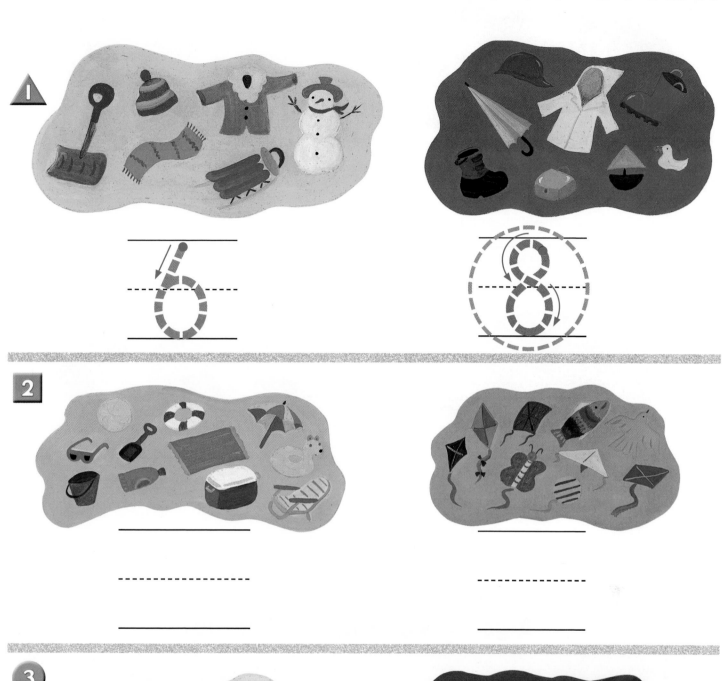

1.

6   8

2.

_____   _____

- - - - - - - - - - - - -   - - - - - - - - - - - - -

_____   _____

3.

_____   _____

- - - - - - - - - - - - -   - - - - - - - - - - - - -

_____   _____

Directions 1–3 Count. Tell which set has more and which has fewer. Write each number.
Circle the greater number.

Chapter 8   **151**

1

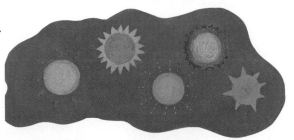

_____

- - - - - - - - - - - - -

_____

_____

- - - - - - - - - - - - -

_____

2

   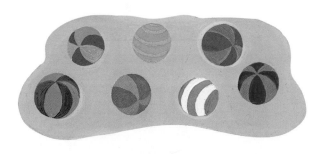

_____

- - - - - - - - - - - - -

_____

_____

- - - - - - - - - - - - -

_____

Algebra Readiness ▶ Functions

3

I More

10	6	9	11

Directions 1–2 Count. Tell which set has more and which has fewer. Write each number. Circle the greater number. **3** Follow the rule to fill in the missing numbers.

At Home Have your child count 10 pieces of pasta and 8 dry beans. Have your child tell which set has more and which has fewer. Have your child tell which number is greater.

152

Name _____ Act It Out

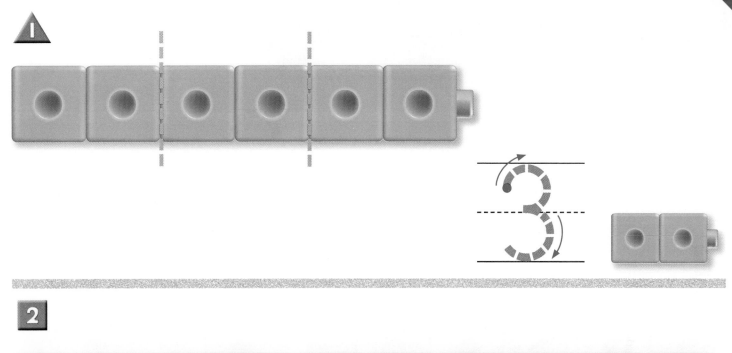

1

2

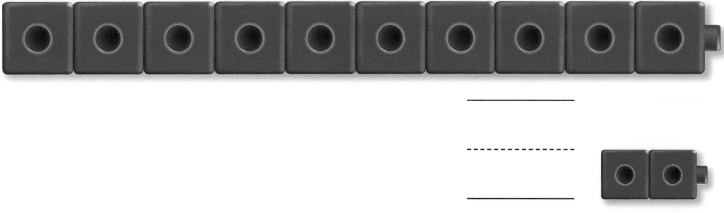

3

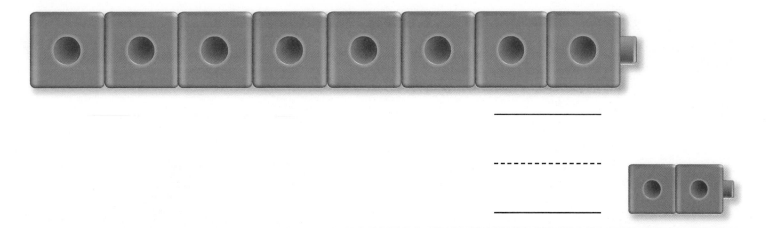

Directions 1–3 Build the cube train. Break it into groups of 2 cubes. Draw lines to show where you broke the train. Write the number of equal groups you made.

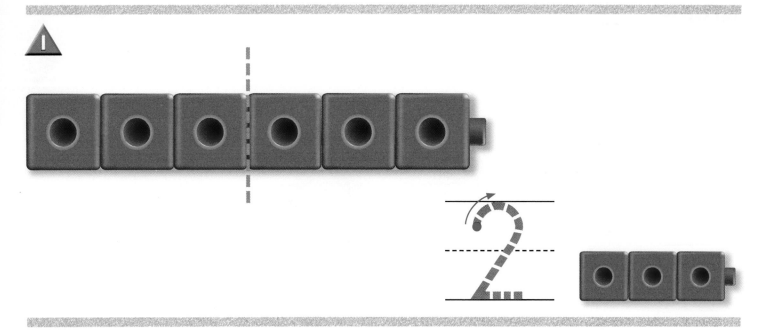

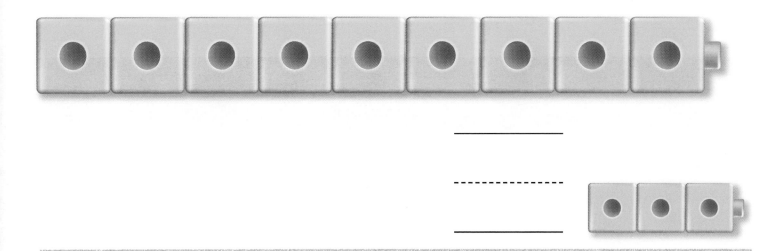

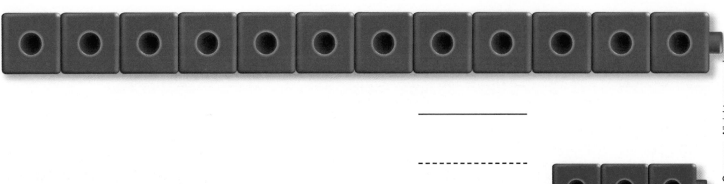

Directions 1–3 Build the cube train. Break it into groups of 3 cubes. Draw lines to show where you broke the train. Write the number of equal groups you made.

At Home Have your child divide 12 paper clips into groups of 2, 3, and 4. Have your child tell how many groups there are.

154

Pitter, Patter Raindrops

This take-home book will help you review concepts you learned in Chapter 8.

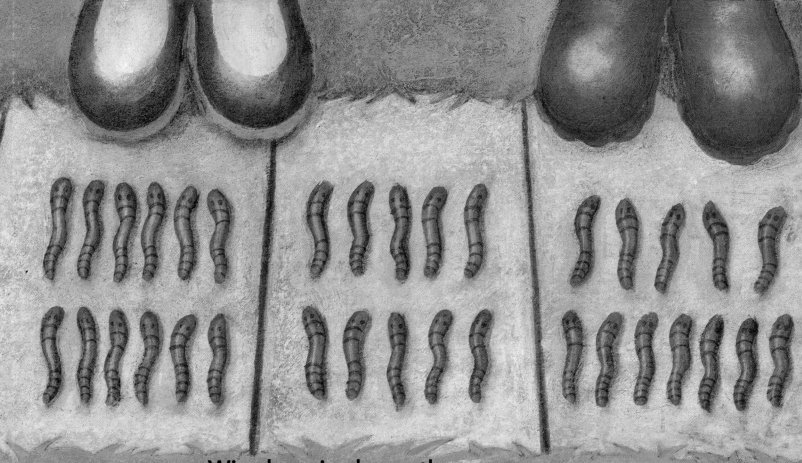

Wiggle, wiggle go the worms.
Which sets of worms show twelve?

Pitter, patter goes the rain.
Which sets of raindrops show seven?

2

1 _____ 3 4 _____ 6

7 8 _____ 10 _____ 12

Splash, splash in the puddles.
Write the missing numbers.

4

5 6 8

6 7 9

Snap, snap go the turtles.
Write the missing numbers.

5

Quack, quack go the ducks.
Which set of ducks has more?

7

Croak, croak go the frogs.
Which sets have 8 frogs?

6

Pitter, patter goes the rain.
Which umbrella has fewer raindrops?

8

_____   _____

7   8   _____   10   _____

2

3

_____   _____

----------------   ----------------

_____   _____

_____

_____

Directions 1 Write the missing numbers. 2 Circle sets of 6 in red. Circle sets of 7 in blue. 3 Count. Write the numbers. Circle the greater number. 4 Build the cube train. Break it into groups of 2 cubes. Draw lines to show where you broke the train. Write the number of equal groups you made.

SPIN AND COUNT!

Start

What You Need

Finish

How to Play 1 Take turns with a partner. 2 Spin the spinner. Move your marker to the first space that has the same number of objects as the number on the spinner. 3 The first player to reach Finish wins.

Name _____

1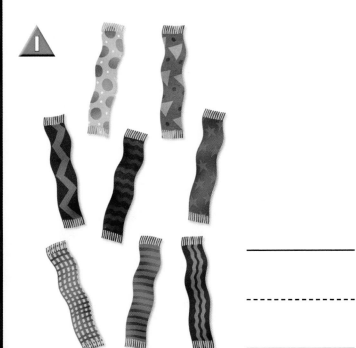

_____

- - - - - - - - - - - - - - - -

_____

2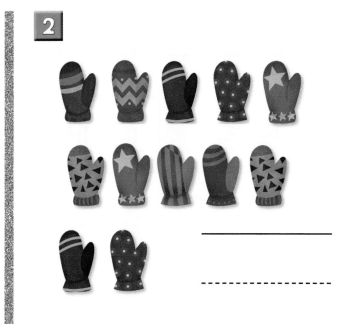

_____

- - - - - - - - - - - - - - - -

_____

3

7   8   9

4

10   11   12

5

_____   _____

- - - - - - - - - -   - - - - - - - - - - -

2   4 _____   8 _____   12

Directions 1–2 Count the items. Write the number. 3–4 Count the items. Circle the number.
5 Look for a pattern. Write the missing numbers.

6

6

7

8

_____   _____

- - - - - - - - - - - [cube]   - - - - - - - - - - [cube]

_____   _____

7

_____   _____

- - - - - - - - - -   - - - - - - - - - -

4   _____   6   7   8   _____

8

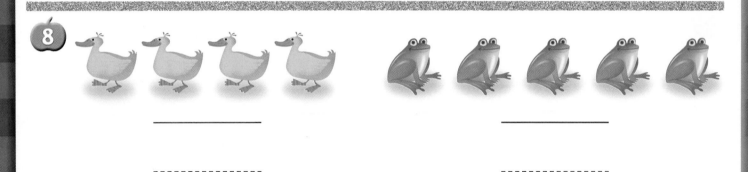

_____   _____

- - - - - - - - - -   - - - - - - - - - -

_____   _____

9

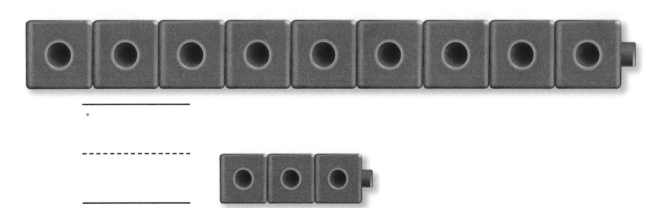

_____

- - - - - - - - - -

_____

Directions **6** Count the cubes. Circle the number. Color some cubes one color and the rest another color. Write the numbers. **7** Write the missing numbers. **8** Count and write the numbers. Circle the greater number. **9** Build the cube train. Break it into groups of 3 cubes. Draw lines to show where you broke the train. Write the number of equal groups.

158

Name _____

Odd and Even Numbers

△1

5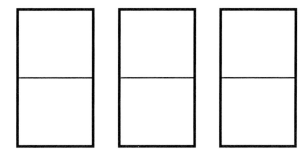

Odd

Even

2

6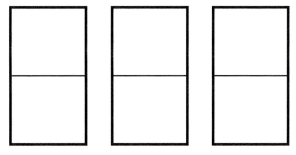

Odd

Even

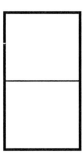

7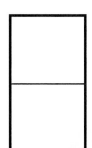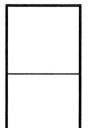

Odd

Even

8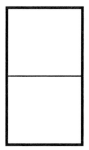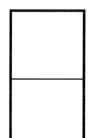

Odd

Even

Directions 1–4 Count out cubes to match the number. Place pairs of cubes in each frame. If each frame has a pair of cubes, circle Even. If not, circle Odd.

WEEKLY WR **READER** Activity Almanac

Unit 4

See page 327.

159

Name _____

_____   _____

- - - - - - - - - -   - - - - - - - - - -

_____   _____

 4

 8

Directions **1** Count and write the number in each set. Circle the set that has fewer. **2** Cross out the item that does not belong in a set of cylinders. **3** Circle the third mouse. **4** Circle the shape that is likely to come next. **5–6** Draw raindrops to show each number.

Photography Credits: 131-132 © Ken Karp. 140(t) © Ken Karp. 140(b) © Siede Preis/PhotoDisc/Getty Images. **Illustration Credits:** 122 © Mircea Catusanu. 123-124 © Promotion Studios. 126 © Mircea Catusanu. 127-128 © John Berg. 129-130 © Mircea Catusanu. 135 © Mircea Catusanu. 137-138 © Mircea Catusanu. Chapter 7 Story © Promotion Studios. 141(t) © Mircea Catusanu. 141(m) © John Berg. 141(b) © Mircea Catusanu. 142(t) © John Berg. 143-144 © Sachiko Yoshikawa. 147-148 © Wallace Keller. 149-152 © Suchiko Yoshikawa. Chapter 8 Story © Wallace Keller. 155(t) © John Berg. 155(m) © Mircea Catusanu. 156 © Sachiko Yoshikawa. 157-158(tl) © Mircea Catusanu. 160(t) © Mircea Catusanu. 60(m) © Wallace Keller.

160

Time and Money

From the Read-Aloud Anthology

Bunny Day

by Rick Walton

illustrated by Paige Miglio

Access Prior Knowledge

This story will help you review

- Times of day

MATH at Home

Dear Family,

We are starting a new unit called Time and Money. In Chapter 9, we will work with calendars and learn how to tell time to the nearest hour on a clock. In Chapter 10, we will identify coins and learn about the value of different coins.

Love, _____

Vocabulary

calendar
A chart showing the days of the week and the months of the year.

clock
A tool to measure and record time.

minute hand

hour hand

3 o'clock

3 o'clock

penny, nickel, dime, quarter
Coins with the value of one cent, five cents, ten cents, and twenty-five cents, respectively.

1¢   5¢   10¢   25¢

Vocabulary Activities

- Have your child use a calendar to name the days of the week and the months of the year.

- Help your child read times to the hour on clocks around your home.

- Let your child sort, identify, and compare different coins. Help your child trade 5 pennies for 1 nickel.

Technology

Visit *Education Place* at
eduplace.com/parents/mw/
for the Math Lingo Game,
e • Glossary, and more.

Literature to Read Together

- **A Chair for My Mother**
by Vera B. Williams
(*Greenwillow Books, 1982*)

- **Just a Minute!**
by Anita Harper
(*Putnam, 1987*)

- **The Pig Is in the Pantry,
The Cat Is on the Shelf**
by Shirley Mozelle
(*Clarion Books, 2000*)

Time

CHAPTER 9

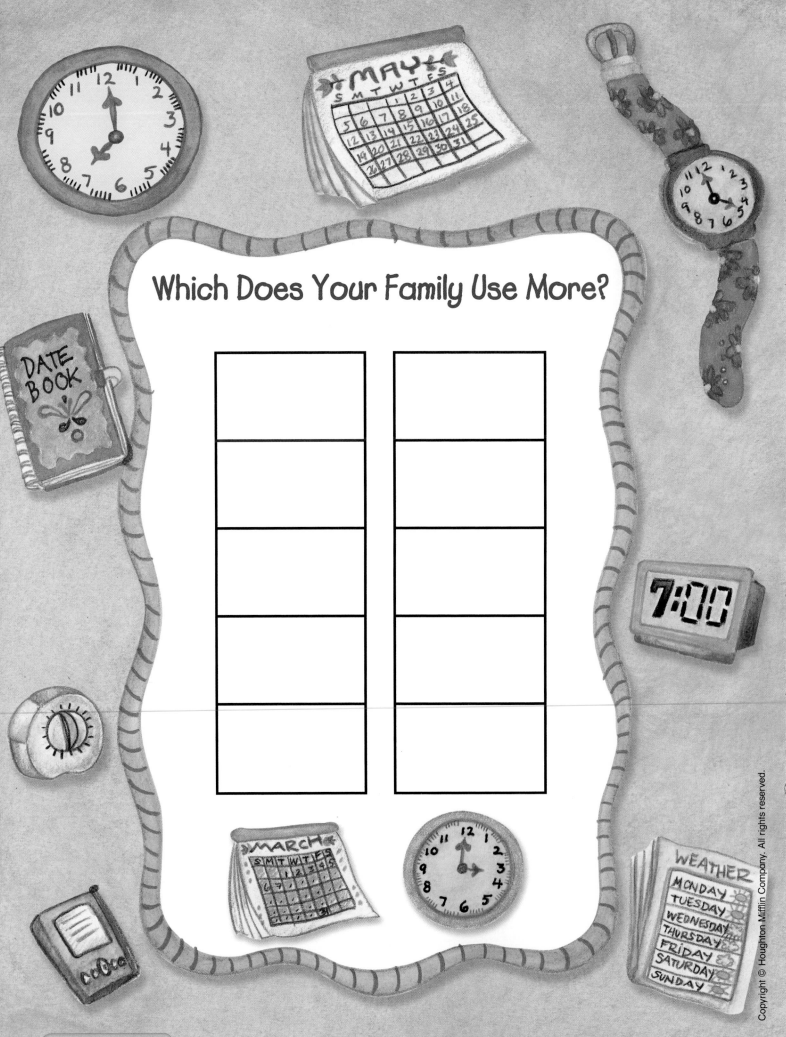

Which Does Your Family Use More?

INVESTIGATION

Directions Think about the things that help us tell time. Ask 5 classmates whether their families use clocks or calendars more. Color a box for each response. Tell about your graph.

Times of Day

1

2

3

Directions Circle the picture that shows: **1** the morning; **2** the afternoon; **3** the evening.

▲ 1

morning

2

afternoon

3

evening

Copyright © Houghton Mifflin Company. All rights reserved.

Directions 1–3 Draw something you do at the time of day pictured.

At Home Name some daily events such as going to school or having dinner. Have your child use the words *day, night, morning, afternoon,* and *evening* to identify the time of day each event happens.

Name _____

Comparing Temperature

Directions 1–3 Color a red frame around the picture that shows a hotter day. Color a blue frame around the picture that shows a colder day.

Chapter 9

167

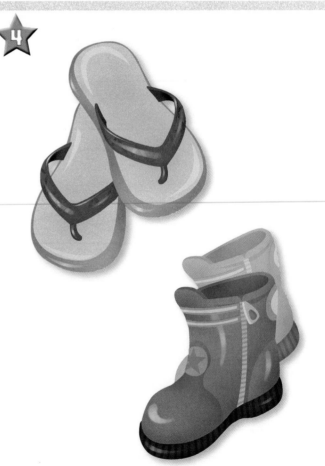

Directions 1–4 Circle in red the clothing worn on a warmer day. Circle in blue the clothing worn on a cooler day.

At Home Help your child use the words *warmer* and *cooler* to compare the temperature during the four seasons. For example, it is cooler in spring than in summer.

Use a Picture

JANUARY

Sunday	Monday	Tuesday	Wednesday	Thursday	Friday	Saturday
	1	2	3	4	5	6
7	8	9	10	11	12	13
14	15	16	17	18	19	20
21	22	23	24	25	26	27
28	29	30	31			

1 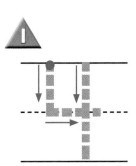 _____ Sundays

2 _____ Tuesdays

3 _____ Fridays

4 _____ days in a week

Directions Count and write the number of: **1** Sundays; **2** Tuesdays; **3** Fridays; **4** days in a week. Circle the first Sunday in red, all the Tuesdays in blue, and the last Friday in green.

APRIL

Sunday	Monday	Tuesday	Wednesday	Thursday	Friday	Saturday
				1	2	3
4	5	6	7	8	9	10
11	12	13	14	15	16	17
18	19	20	21	22	23	24
25	26	27	28	29	30	

1

_____

- - - - - - - - - - - - - - -

_____ Mondays

2

_____

- - - - - - - - - - - - - - -

_____ Thursdays

3

_____

- - - - - - - - - - - - - - -

_____ Wednesdays

4

_____

- - - - - - - - - - - - - - -

_____ Saturdays

Directions Write the number of: 1 Mondays;
2 Thursdays; 3 Wednesdays; 4 Saturdays. Circle the
second Monday in red, all the Thursdays in blue, the third
Wednesday in green, and the last Saturday in yellow.

At Home Help your child point to and read the
numbers on this month's calendar. Have your child
find different days such as the first Tuesday.

170

Name _____

Directions 1–3 Underline the activity you predict will take more time. Do the activities. Circle in red the activity that took more time. Circle in blue the activity that took less time.

 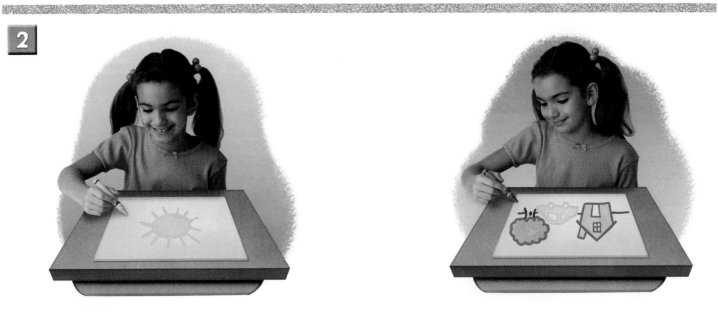

Directions 1–2 Circle in red the activity that takes more time. Circle in blue the activity that takes less time. 3 Circle the picture that shows the afternoon. 4 Circle the clothing worn on a warmer day.

At Home Let your child compare two home activities. Talk about which takes more time and which takes less time.

 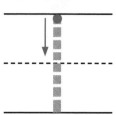 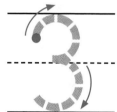

_____   _____   _____

- - - - - - - - - -   - - - - - - - - - -   - - - - - - - - - -

_____   _____   _____

Directions 1–2 Write the numbers *1, 2,* and *3* to show the order of events from first to last.

_____   _____   _____

- - - - - - - - - - -   - - - - - - - - - - -   - - - - - - - - - - -

_____   _____   _____

_____   _____   _____

- - - - - - - - - - -   - - - - - - - - - - -   - - - - - - - - - - -

_____   _____   _____

Problem Solving ▷ Visual Thinking

Directions 1-2 Write the numbers *1, 2,* and *3* to show the order of events from first to last. **3** Circle the one that is likely to come next.

At Home Have your child tell you some events of his or her day in order. Encourage your child to use the words *first, next,* and *last.*

174

_____

_____ o'clock

Directions Write the missing numbers on the clock. Write the time shown on the clock.

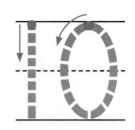 o'clock

_____

_____ o'clock

_____

_____ o'clock

_____

_____ o'clock

_____

_____ o'clock

Directions 1–5 Write the time shown on the clock.

At Home Fold this page lengthwise so only the clocks are showing. Point to each clock and have your child tell you the time that is shown.

More Time to the Hour

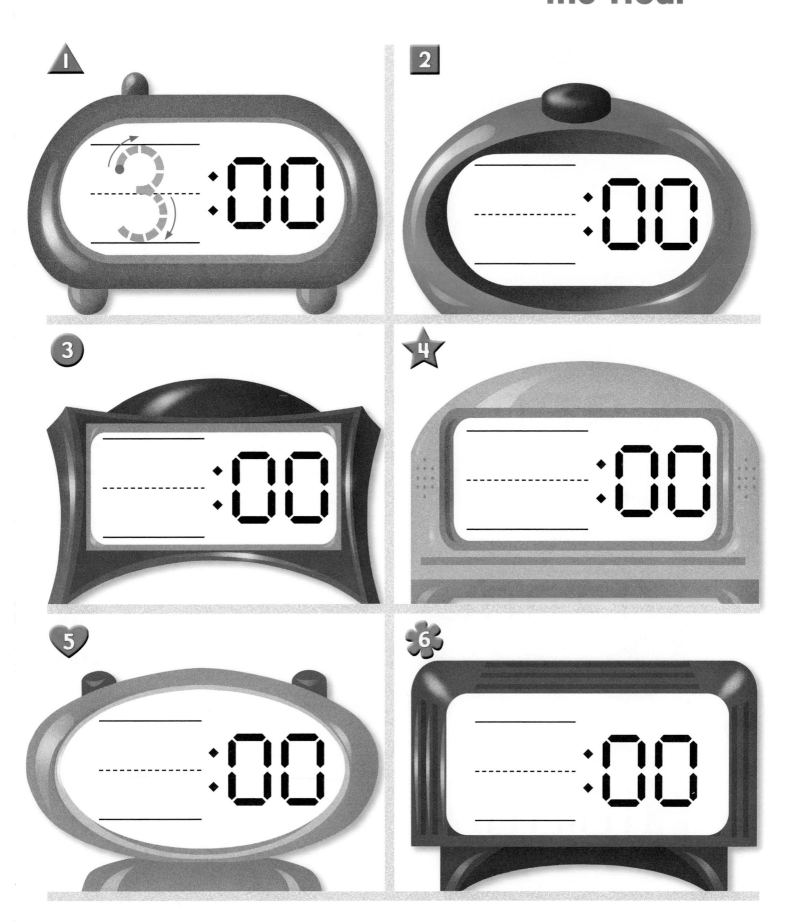

Directions Show the following times on the clocks: **1** 3 o'clock, **2** 7 o'clock, **3** 4 o'clock, **4** 11 o'clock, **5** 2 o'clock, and **6** 9 o'clock.

1  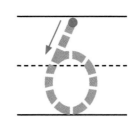 _____ o'clock

2  _____ o'clock

3  _____ o'clock

4  _____ o'clock

5  _____ o'clock

Directions 1–5 Write the time shown on the clock.

At Home Have your child point to each clock and tell you the time. Talk about things that he or she might do at each time shown.

Compare Digital and Analog Clocks

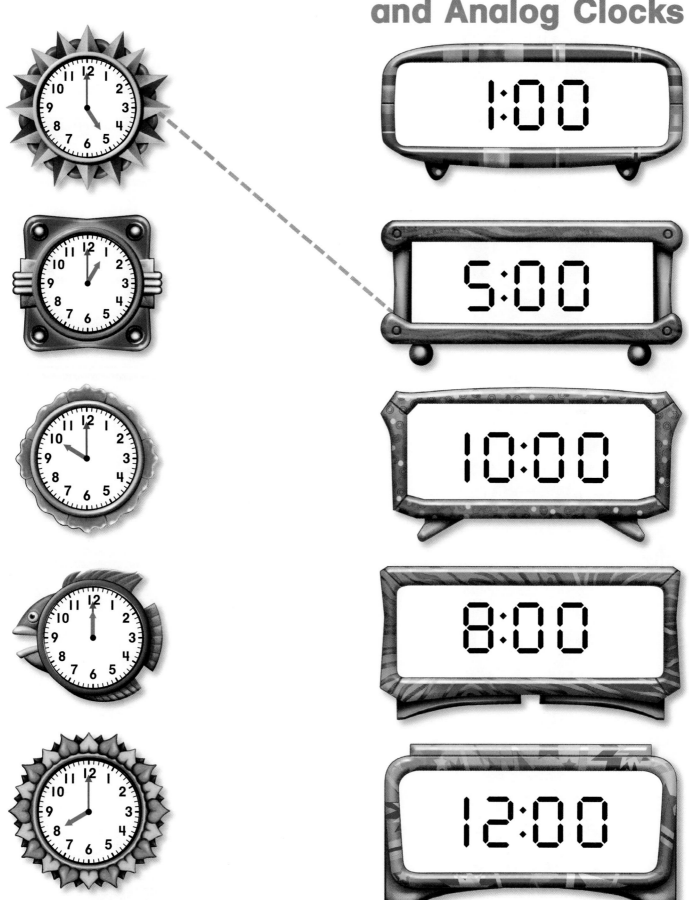

Directions Draw lines to match the clocks that show the same time.

1

3:00

2

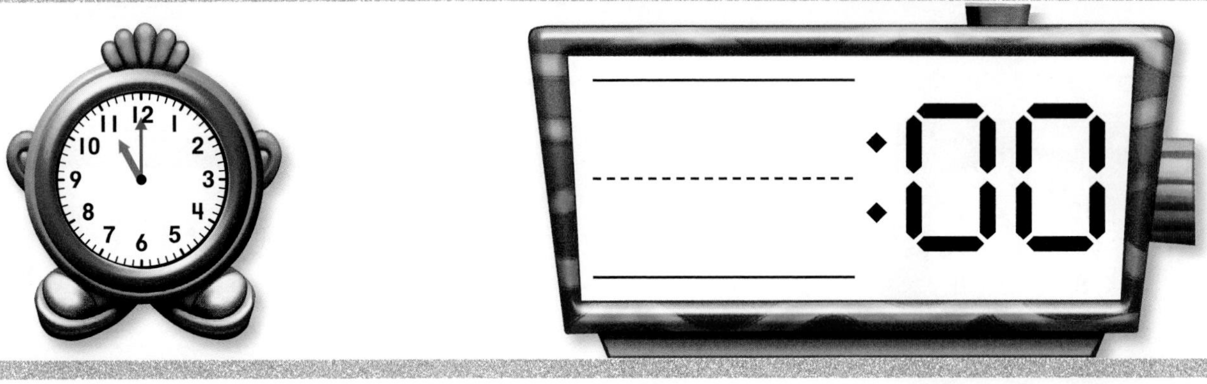

:00

3

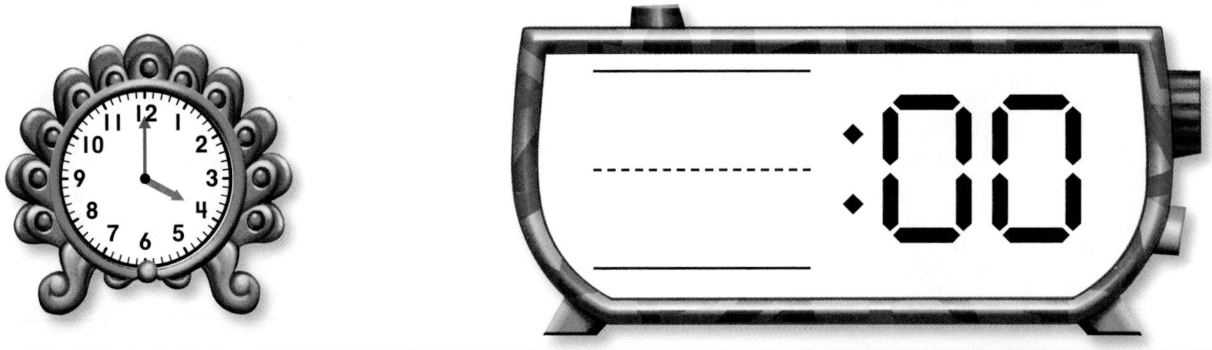

:00

4

:00

5

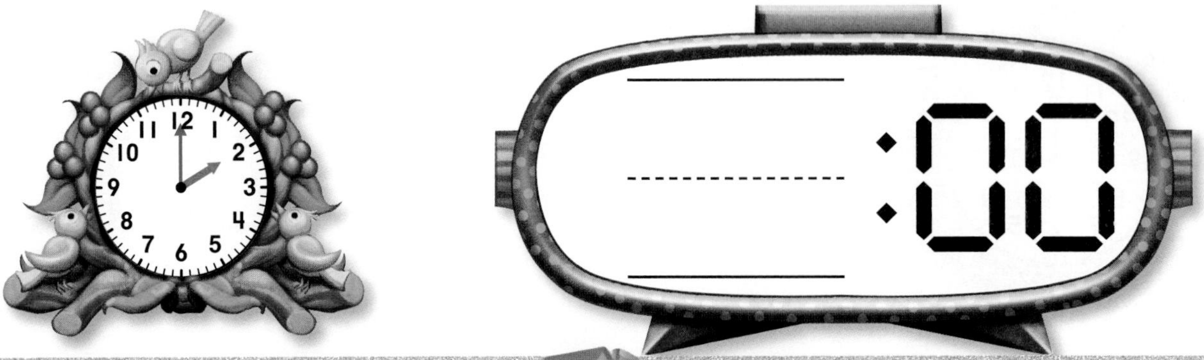

:00

Directions 1–5 Write the time on the digital clock to match the time shown.

At Home Draw attention to clocks in your home and neighborhood. Help your child read times on the hour.

Polly Piglet's Day

This take-home book will help you review concepts you learned in Chapter 9.

MARCH

	Thursday	Friday	Saturday
	1	2	3 CARLOS
	8		10
	16	17	
28			

MILK

cereal

Yesterday was Friday.
What day is it today?

It is time for Polly Piglet to get up.
Is it morning, afternoon, or evening?

2

Carlos Cow has come to play.
Is it cooler inside or outside?

4

Polly and Carlos play with blocks.
Which tower took more time to make?

5

Polly says goodbye to Carlos.
What time is it?

_____ :00

7

It is lunchtime.

What happens first, next, and last?

6

Polly loves bedtime stories.
What time is it?

_____ o'clock

8

Name _____

1

2

3

---------------   ---------------   ---------------

_____   _____   _____

4

5

March

Sunday	Monday	Tuesday	Wednesday	Thursday	Friday	Saturday
			1	2	3	4
5	6	7	8	9	10	11
12	13	14	15	16	17	18
19	20	21	22	23	24	25
26	27	28	29	30	31	

Directions 1 Circle the picture that shows the afternoon. 2 Circle the activity that takes more time.
3 Write *1*, *2*, and *3* to show the order of events from first to last. 4 Write the time. 5 Circle the last
Tuesday in red. Circle the first Thursday in blue.

Directions Follow the bus route to school. Circle in red the group that will get on first. Circle in blue the group that will get on next. Circle in green the group that will get on last. Talk about the community helpers along the way.

182

Money

LEMONADE

2¢
5¢
10¢

Coin tally

Coin	How Many
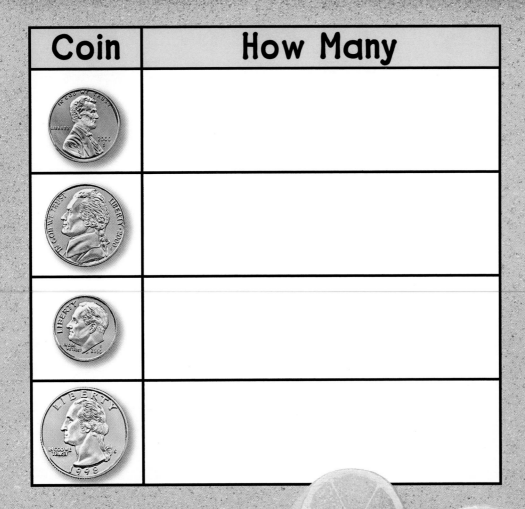	

INVESTIGATION

Directions Make a tally chart of the coins. Cross out each coin as you make a tally mark in the chart. Tell what you know about the different coins.

Name_____ **Penny**

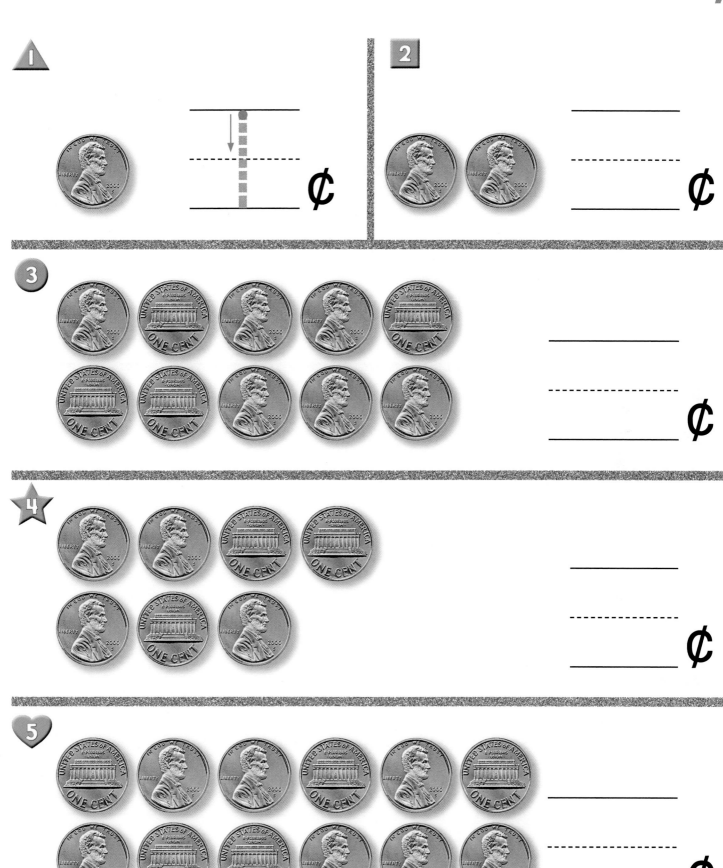

Directions 1–5 Write the number of cents.

Chapter 10   185

1

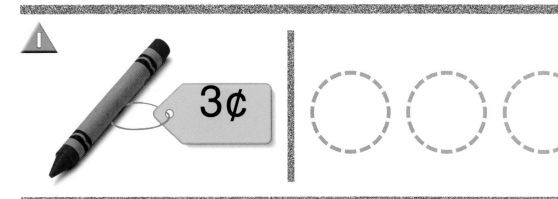

3¢

2

2¢

3

5¢

4

8¢

5

6¢

Directions: 1–5 Use pennies to show each price.
Draw the pennies.

At Home Have your child separate the pennies
from a handful of coins. Let your child use pennies
to count out groups of 5¢, 8¢, 10¢, and 12¢.

Name_____ Nickel

 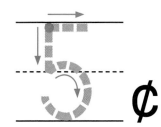 ¢

  _____
- - - - - - - - -
_____ ¢

  _____
- - - - - - - - -
_____ ¢

   _____
- - - - - - - - -
_____ ¢

     _____
- - - - - - - - -
_____ ¢

Directions 1–5 Write the number of cents.

1

6¢   **7¢**   8¢

2

1¢   5¢   10¢

3

4¢   5¢   9¢

4

8¢   7¢   4¢

Directions 1–4 Circle the price tag that matches the number of cents.

At Home Have your child identify all the nickels in a handful of coins. Then have your child make and count groups of coins that include 1 nickel and up to 5 pennies.

Name_____ **Dime**

Directions Circle the groups that show 10¢. Use pennies to make all groups show 10¢.
Draw the pennies you used.

1

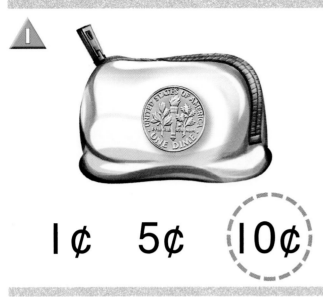

1¢   5¢   (10¢)

2

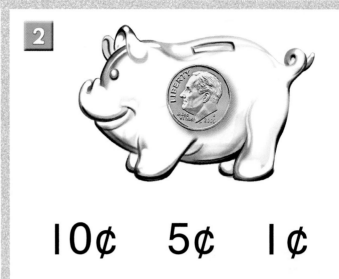

10¢   5¢   1¢

3

6¢   10¢   5¢

4

8¢   9¢   10¢

5

_____
- - - - - - -
_____ ¢

6

_____
- - - - - - -
_____ ¢

Directions 1–4 Circle the number of cents. 5–6 Write the number of cents.

At Home Have your child separate the dimes from a handful of coins. Then have your child make groups of pennies that equal 10 cents.

Directions Circle all the quarters. Count and write the number of quarters.

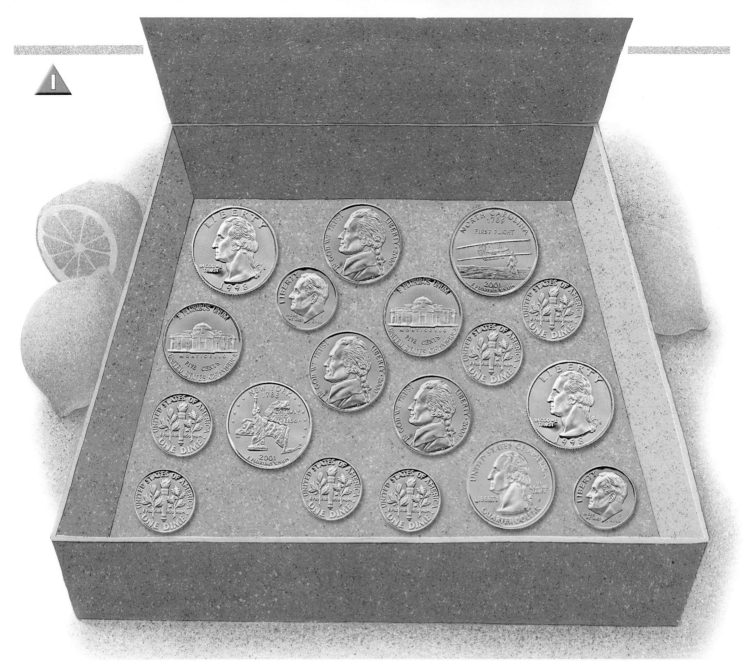

Problem Solving ▸ Number Sense

Directions ┃ Circle the quarters in red, the dimes in blue, and the nickels in yellow. **2–3** Circle the group that will buy more.

At Home Have your child separate the quarters from a handful of coins. Talk about how a quarter differs from both a dime and a nickel.

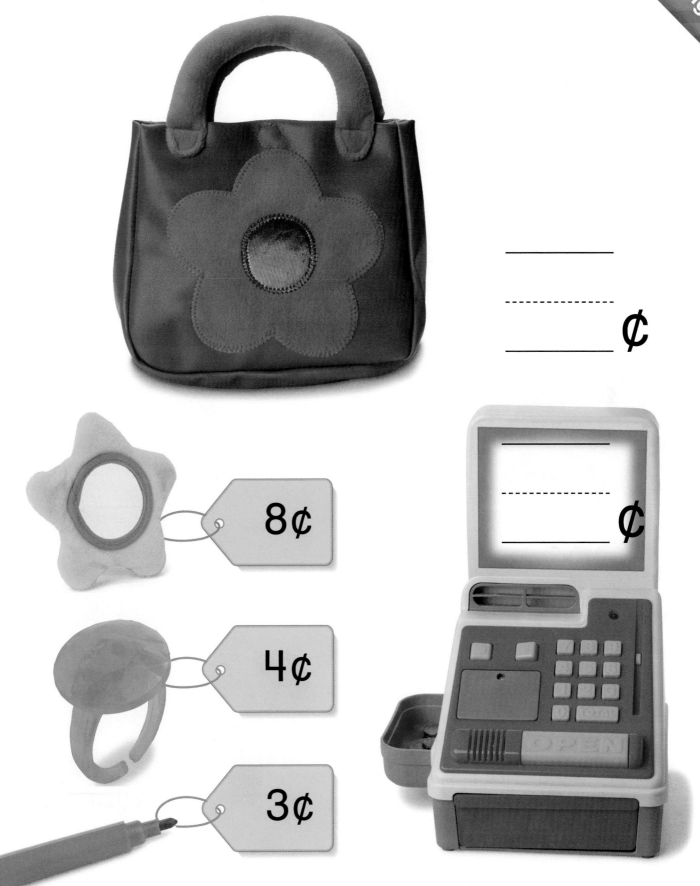

_____
- - - - - - - - - -
_____ ¢

8¢

4¢

3¢

_____
- - - - - - - - - -
_____ ¢

Directions Place 10 pennies on the purse. Circle an item you want to buy. Move that many cents to the cash register. Write how much you spent. Write what you have left in the purse.

Chapter 10

193

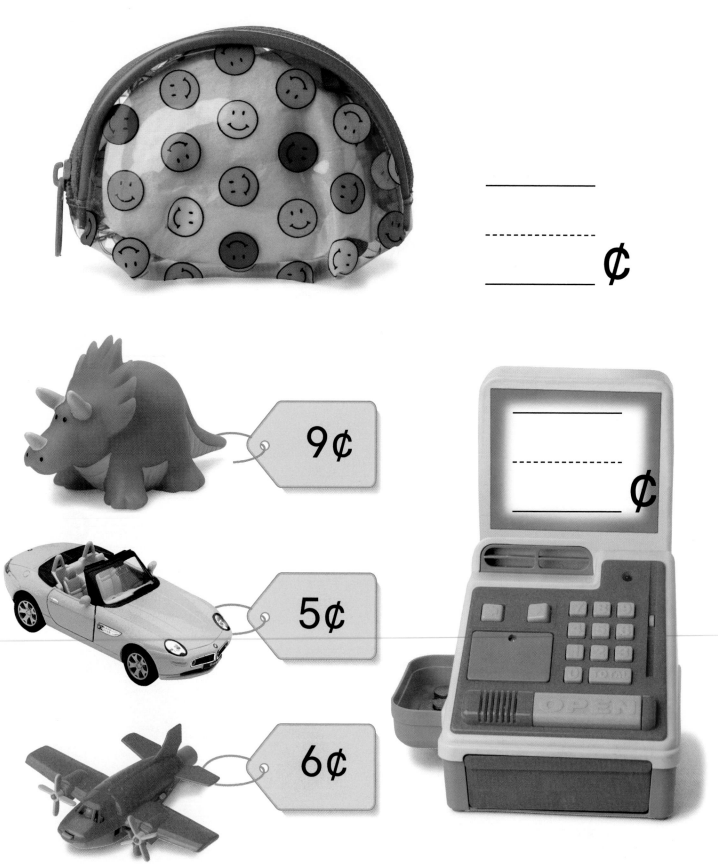

_____
- - - - - - - - -
_____ ¢

9¢

5¢

6¢

Directions Place 10 pennies on the coin purse. Circle an item you want to buy. Move that many cents to the cash register. Write how much you spent. Write what you have left in the coin purse.

At Home Have your child use 10 pennies to act out purchasing different items. Have your child tell how much he or she spent and how much is left.

194

Sam's Coins

This take-home book will help you review concepts you learned in Chapter 10.

1

Sam finds more coins.

Name the coins.

3

Grandpa hides coins for Sam to find.
Name the coins.

2

Sam counts his pennies.
Write the number of cents. _____ ¢

4

Grandpa holds a coin.
Write the number of cents.

_____
¢

Sam buys a pencil.
Which coins show 8¢?

Grandpa holds more coins.
Write the number of cents.

_____ ¢

6

Grandpa gives Sam a bank.
Which coin does Sam save?

8

Name_____

1

_____
- - - - - - - - - - -
_____ ¢

2

_____
- - - - - - - - - - -
_____ ¢

3

4

5¢

_____
- - - - - - - - - - -
_____ ¢

Directions 1–2 Write the number of cents. 3 Circle the pennies in red, the nickels in blue, the dimes in yellow, and the quarters in green. 4 Circle the pennies used to buy the item. Write the cents left.

MONEY MATCH

What You Need

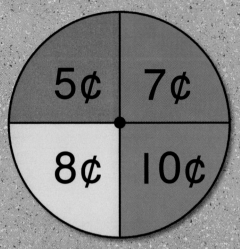

5¢	7¢
8¢	10¢

How to Play 1 Take turns with a partner. 2 Spin the spinner. Place a counter on a space that shows that number of cents. 3 Play until all the spaces are covered.

196

Name _____

2

3

_____

- - - - - - - - - - - - - -

_____ o'clock

APRIL

Sunday	Monday	Tuesday	Wednesday	Thursday	Friday	Saturday
					1	2
3	4	5	6	7	8	9
10	11	12	13	14	15	16
17	18	19	20	21	22	23
24	25	26	27	28	29	30

_____

- - - - - - - - - - - - - -

_____

Directions 1 Circle the picture that shows morning. 2 Circle the activity that takes less time.
3 Write the time. 4 Circle the first Monday in red. Circle the first day of the month in blue.
Write the number of days in a week.

_____

- - - - - - - - - - - -

_____ ¢

_____

- - - - - - - - - - - -

_____ ¢

7¢

_____

- - - - - - - - - - - -

_____ ¢

Directions 5 Circle the dime. 6 Circle the quarter. 7–8 Write the number of cents.
9 Circle the pennies used to buy the item. Write the cents left.

198

Name _____

1

Dollar

2

Directions 1 Discuss the dollar coins and bills. 2 Circle the
dollars. Cross out the ones that are not dollars.

WEEKLY WR READER® Activity Almanac

Unit 5   See page 328.   **199**

1

2

3

_____

- - - - - - - - - - - - - -

_____

4
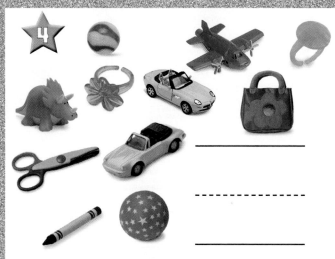

_____

- - - - - - - - - - - - - -

_____

5

_____

- - - - - - - - - - - - - -

_____ o'clock

6

_____

- - - - - - - - - - - - - -

_____ ¢

Directions 1 Circle the triangles. 2 Circle the cylinders. 3–4 Count. Write the number.
5 Write the time. 6 Write the number of cents.

Photography Credits: 165(ml), 200(2tl) © C Squared Studios/PhotoDisc/Getty Images. 186(tm), 200(4mbl) © Joe Atlas/Brand X Pictures/PictureQuest. 165, 171–172, 181, 186, 193–195, 197–198, 200(remaining images) © Ken Karp. **Illustration Credits:** 162(tl), 163–164, 172(b), 182 © Esther Szegedy. 162(b), 165–166, 171, 172(t); 172(m), 179–180, 181, 188–90, 195, 197–199 © Mark and Rosemary Jarman. 167–170, 173–178, Chapter 9 Story, 200 © Mircea Catusanu. 183–184, 191–192, 196 © Dagmar Fehlau. Chapter 10 Story © Elizabeth Sayles.

1 2 3 4 5 6 7 8 9 – WC – 12 11 10 09 08 07 06 05 04 03

Name _____

Directions 1–4 Circle the taller one. Underline the shorter one. 5 Circle the longer one.
Underline the shorter one.

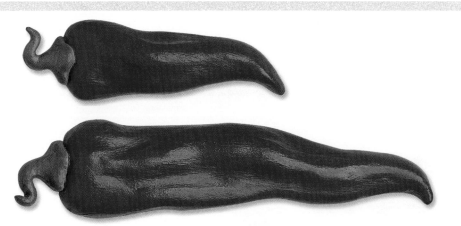

Directions 1–4 Circle the longer one. Underline the shorter one.

At Home Help your child find items both taller and shorter than he or she is. Then help your child find items that are longer or shorter than his or her arm.

206

Name _____ **Order by Length**

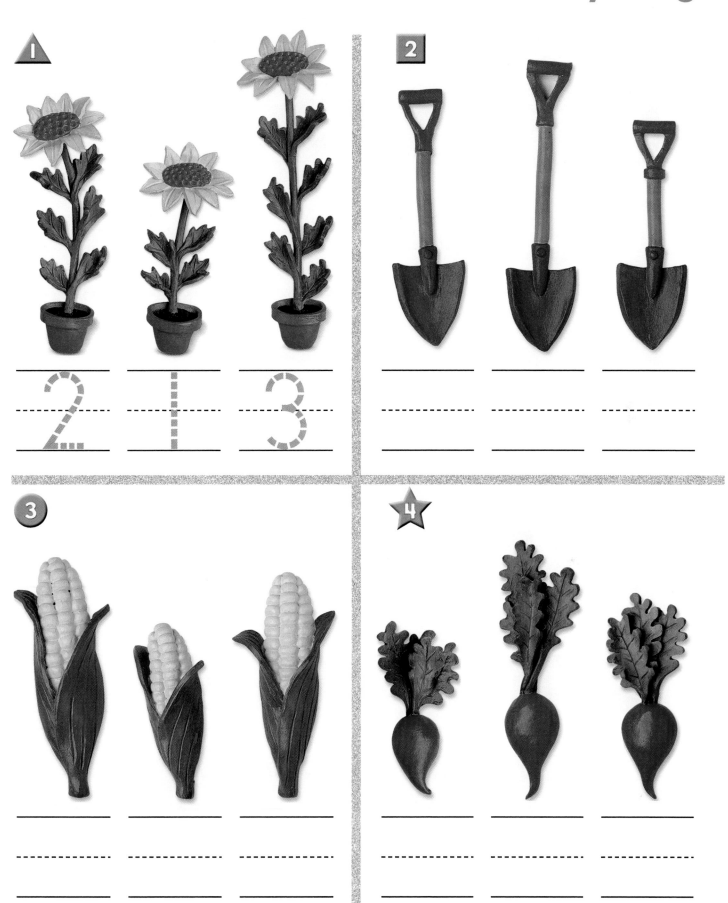

▲ 1

2

3

★ 4

2   1   3

Directions 1–4 Write the numbers *1*, *2*, and *3* to order the items from shortest to tallest.

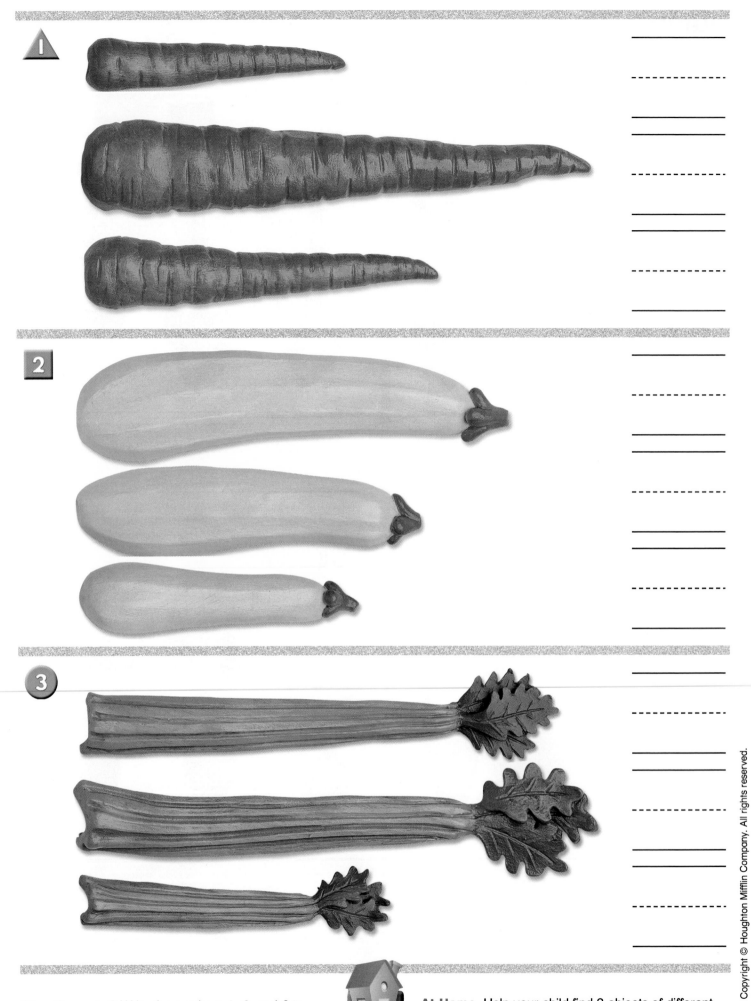

Directions 1–3 Write the numbers *1*, *2*, and *3* to order the items from shortest to longest.

At Home Help your child find 3 objects of different lengths and put them in order from shortest to longest.

208

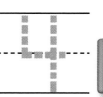

about _____

2

about _____

3

about _____

4

about _____

Directions 1–4 Use cubes to measure the length. Record the length.

1

about _____

2

about _____

Directions 1–2 Use cubes to measure the length. Record the length. 3 Circle the taller one. Underline the shorter one. 4 Write the numbers *1*, *2*, and *3* to order the items from shortest to longest.

At Home Draw lines of different lengths on paper. Have your child use paper clips or pennies to measure each length and tell which is longer or shorter.

Name _____ Estimate and Measure Length

⚠ 1

Estimate

about _____ 🔲

Measure

about _____ 🔲

2

Estimate

about _____ 🔲

Measure

about _____ 🔲

3

Estimate

about _____ 🔲

Measure

about _____ 🔲

Directions 1–3 Estimate how many cubes long. Measure. Record the length. Compare the measurement to the estimate.

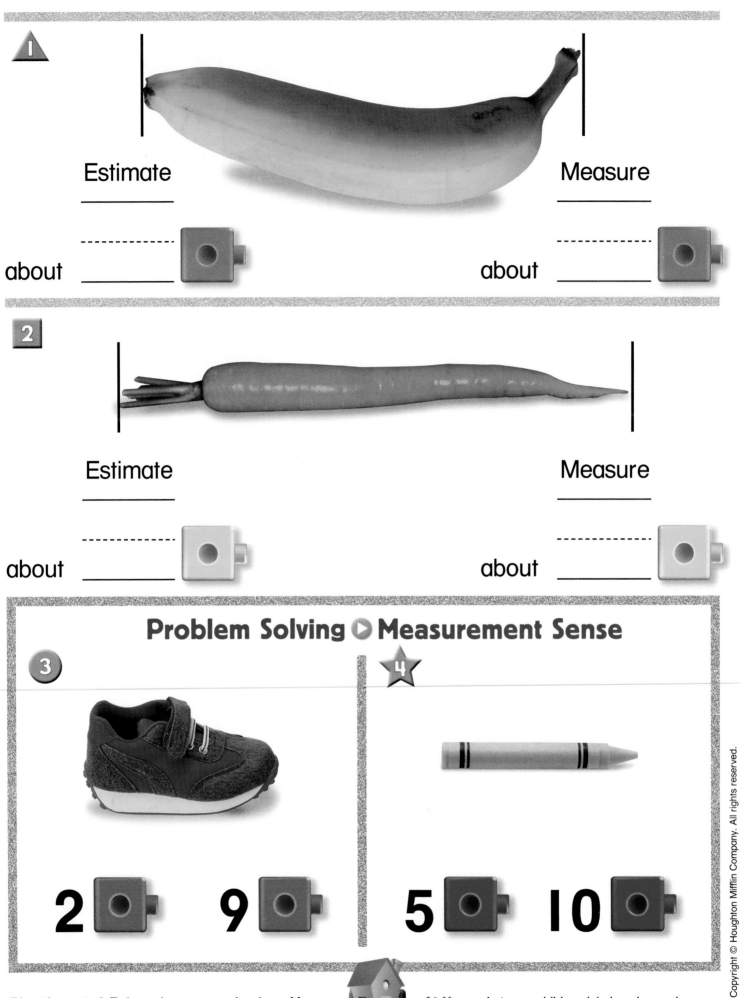

1

Estimate

about _____

Measure

about _____

2

Estimate

about _____

Measure

about _____

Problem Solving ▶ Measurement Sense

3

2   **9**

4

5   **10**

Directions 1–2 Estimate how many cubes long. Measure. Record the length. Compare the measurement to the estimate. 3–4 Circle the most likely length of the real item.

At Home Let your child explain how he or she estimated and measured the lengths above.

212

Name _____ **Act It Out**

Estimate   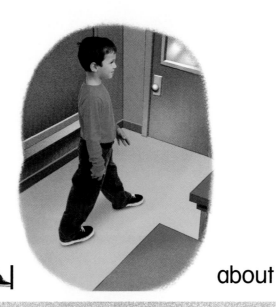   Measure

_____   _____

about _____   about _____

2

Estimate       Measure

_____   _____

about _____   about _____

3

Estimate      Measure

_____   _____

about _____   about _____

Directions Estimate the number of: **1** giant steps to cross the classroom; **2** forearms long the board is;
3 hand spans long the table is. Measure and record. Compare measurements to estimates.

▲ 1

Estimate

_____

about _____

Measure

_____

about _____

2

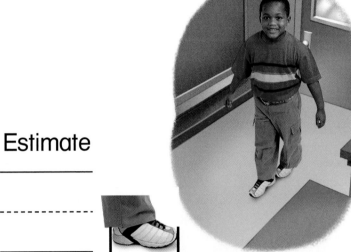

Estimate

_____

about _____

Measure

_____

about _____

3

Estimate

_____

about _____

Measure

_____

about _____

Directions Estimate the number of: **1** hand spans wide the door is; **2** foot lengths long the board is; **3** hand spans high the bookcase is. Measure and record. Compare measurements to estimates.

At Home Let your child explain how he or she estimated and measured in this lesson. Estimate and measure some similar lengths at home.

Cali, Sal, and Andy's Garden Adventure

This take-home book will help you review concepts you learned in Chapter 11.

Next, Cali meets Andy Ant.
Who is shorter?

3

Cali meets Sal Snake.
Who is longer?

2

Up the vines they race.
Which vine is taller?

4

The cornstalks are tall.
Which is the tallest?

The beans taste good.
Which bean is the longest?

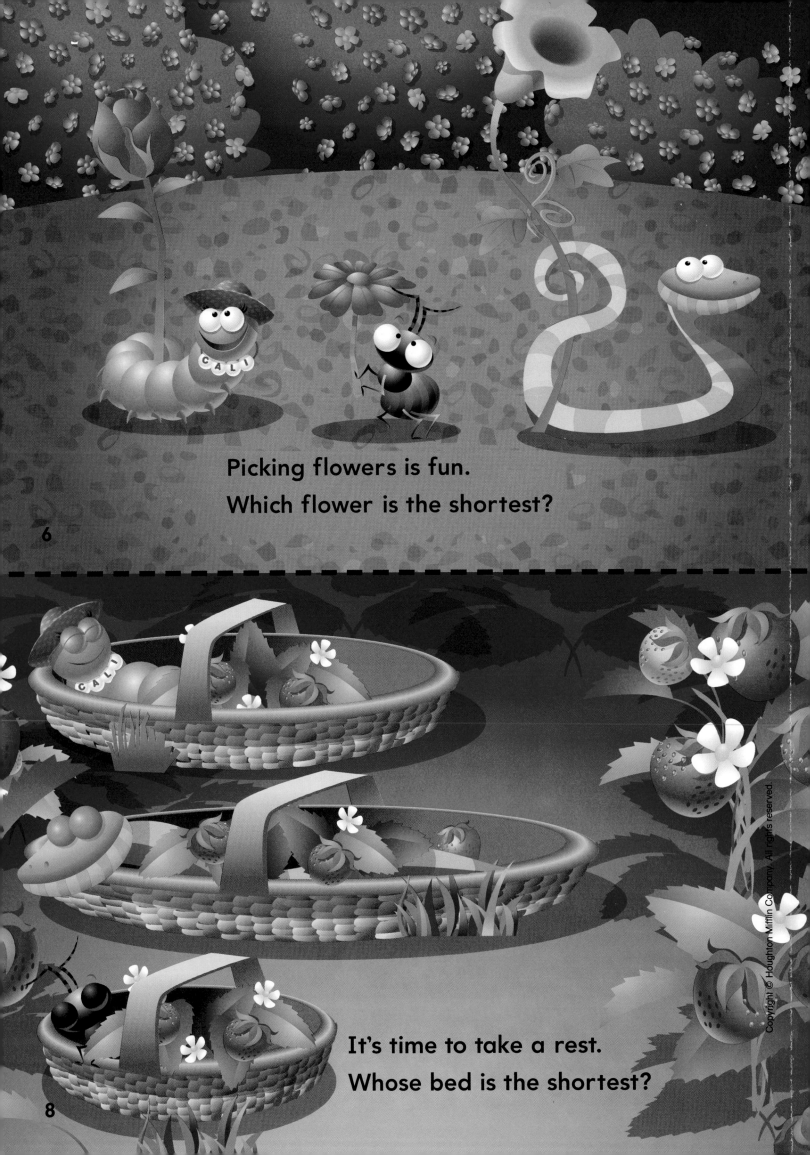

Picking flowers is fun.
Which flower is the shortest?

6

It's time to take a rest.
Whose bed is the shortest?

8

Name _____

1

2

_____
- - - - - - - - -
_____

_____
- - - - - - - - -
_____

_____
- - - - - - - - -
_____

3

about _____

4

about _____

5

Estimate

Measure

_____
- - - - - - -

about _____

_____
- - - - - - -

about _____

Directions **1** Circle the taller one. Underline the shorter one. **2** Write the numbers *1*, *2*, and *3* to order the items from shortest to longest. **3–4** Use cubes to measure the length. Record the length. **5** Estimate how many cubes long. Measure. Record the length.

Chapter 11

Directions Compare the plants in the picture. Tell how they are alike and different. **1** Circle in red the plant that is the tallest. **2** Circle in blue the plant with the thickest stem. **3** Circle in yellow the plant with the smallest leaves.

216

Weight and Capacity

Big or Small?

big						
small						

INVESTIGATION

Directions Circle in red all the big items. Circle in blue all the small items. Color one box to match each item you circled. Tell about your graph.

Directions 1–4 Circle the heavier one. Underline the lighter one. 5 Circle the two that are about the same weight.

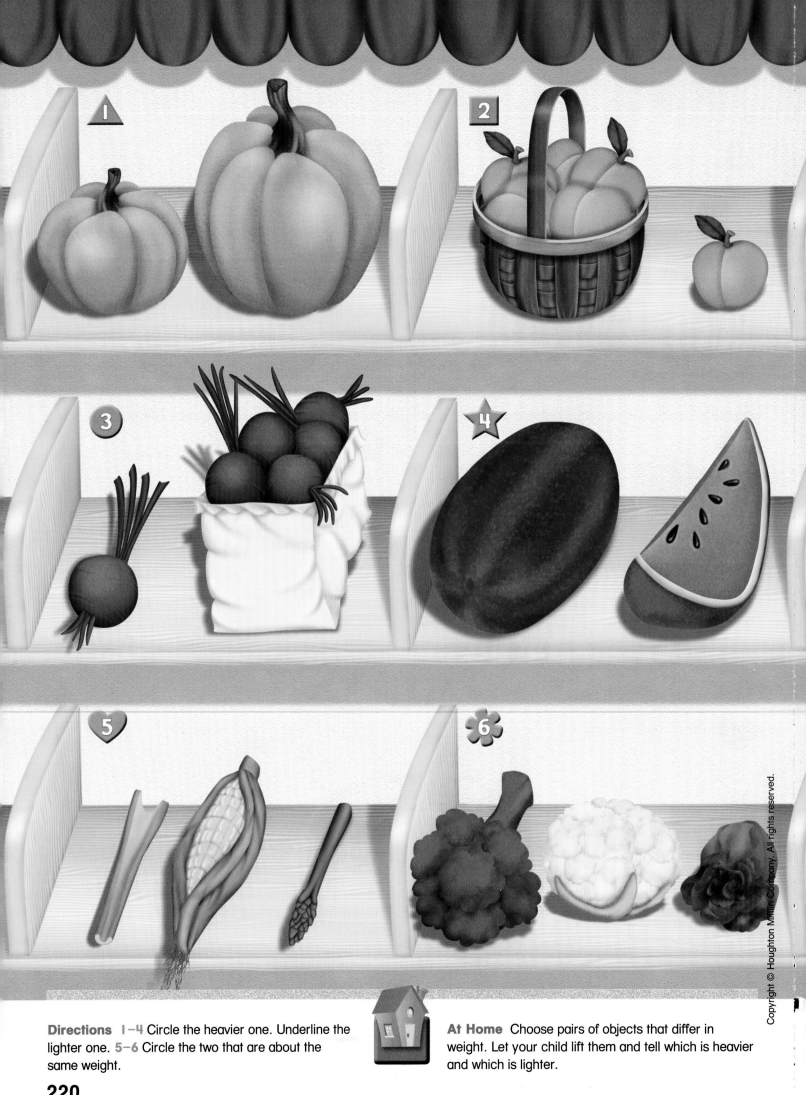

Directions 1–4 Circle the heavier one. Underline the lighter one. 5–6 Circle the two that are about the same weight.

At Home Choose pairs of objects that differ in weight. Let your child lift them and tell which is heavier and which is lighter.

220

Gardening Pals

This take-home book will help you review concepts you learned in Chapter 12.

They pick fruit.
Draw a fruit that is heavier.

Tracy and Beth plant seeds.
Which is lighter, the seeds or the pot?

2

They pick vegetables.
Which one is the lightest?

4

They water the plants.
Which watering can holds more?

5

They pick bunches of grapes.
Which basket holds the least?

7

They fill many bowls.
Which bowl holds the most?

6

Tracy and Beth work together.
Draw a pail that holds less.

8

Name _____

Chapter Review / Test

_____   _____   _____

- -

_____   _____   _____

about **2**

about **12**

Directions 1 Circle the heavier one. Underline the lighter one. 2 Circle the one that holds more.
Underline the one that holds less. 3 Write *1*, *2*, and *3* to order the items from lightest to heaviest.
4 Circle the number of cups needed to fill the can. 5 Circle the lighter one.

LONGER, SHORTER, SAME?

What You Need

How to Play 1 Take turns with a partner. 2 Roll the number cube and move your cube train that number of spaces. 3 Use your cube train to measure. If the animal is longer, move ahead 1 space. If the animal is shorter, go back 1 space. If it is the same length, stay.

236

I

2

3

about _____

4

Estimate

about _____

Measure

about _____

Directions: I Circle the longer one. Underline the shorter one. 2 Write the numbers _I_, _2_, and _3_ to order the items from shortest to longest. 3 Use cubes to measure the length. Record the length. 4 Estimate how many cubes long. Measure. Record the length.

_____   _____   _____

---------------   ---------------   ---------------

_____   _____   _____

Directions: **5** Circle the heavier one. Underline the lighter one. **6** Circle the one that holds more.
Underline the one that holds less. **7** Write *1*, *2*, and *3* to order the items from the one that holds the
least to the one that holds the most. **8** Circle the heaviest one. Underline the lightest one.

Name _____

Measure With a Ruler

1

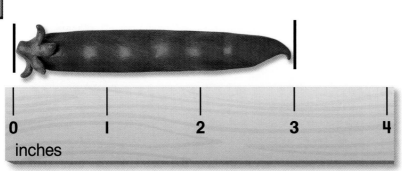

0   1   2   3   4
inches

_____

- - - - - - - - - -

about _____ inches

2

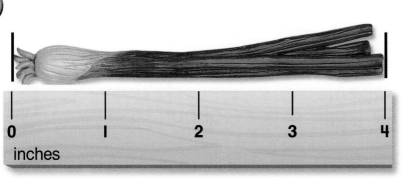

0   1   2   3   4
inches

_____

- - - - - - - - - -

about _____ inches

3

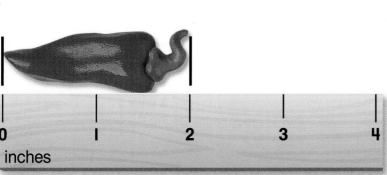

0   1   2   3   4
inches

_____

- - - - - - - - - -

about _____ inches

4

0   1   2   3   4
inches

_____

- - - - - - - - - -

about _____ inches

Directions 1–4 Find the length. Write the number of inches.

WEEKLY WR READER® Activity Almanac

See page 329.

Name _____

△ 1

2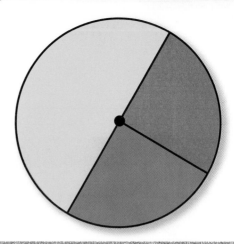

3

_____

- - - - - - - - - - - - -

_____

_____

- - - - - - - - - - - - -

_____

_____

- - - - - - - - - - - - -

_____

★ 4

_____

- - - - - - - - - - - - -

about _____

5

_____   _____

- - - - - - - - - - - - -   - - - - - - - - - - - - -

1   3   _____   **7**   _____   **1 1**

Directions: 1 Circle the quarters. 2 Put an X on the color you are most likely to spin. 3 Write *1*, *2*, and *3* to show the order of events from first to last. 4 Use cubes to measure the length. Record the length. 5 Look for a pattern. Write the missing numbers.

Addition and Subtraction

From the Read-Aloud Anthology

QUACK and COUNT

by
Keith Baker

Access Prior Knowledge

This story will help you review

- Counting
- Names for numbers

MATH at Home

Dear Family,

We are starting a new unit called Addition and Subtraction. In Chapter 13, we will add two groups to find a sum. In Chapter 14, we will subtract a small group from a larger group to find what is left. We will also learn how addition and subtraction are related.

Love, _____

Vocabulary

add
Putting groups together to find the total or the sum.

6 ducks in all

subtract
Taking away to find the difference.

3 ducks are left

addition sentence
An equation such as

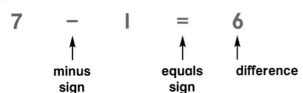

3	+	2	=	5
↑	↑		↑	↑
	plus sign		equals sign	sum

subtraction sentence
An equation such as

7	−	l	=	6
↑		↑		↑
minus sign		equals sign		difference

Vocabulary Activities

- Help your child recognize addition and subtraction situations. (5 people and 1 joins them; 6 in all. Have 5 crackers. Eat 2; 3 crackers are left.)

- Encourage your child to tell addition and subtraction stories, using objects such as pennies or dry beans. Have your child say the number sentence.

 Technology
Visit *Education Place* at
eduplace.com/parents/mw/
for the Math Lingo Game,
e • Glossary, and more.

Literature to Read Together

- **Splash!**
by Ann Jonas
(Mulberry Books, 1997)

- **More Bugs? Less Bugs?**
by Don L. Curry
(Capstone, 2000)

- **Catch That Goat!**
by Polly Alakija
(Barefoot Books, 2002)

Addition

INVESTIGATION

Directions Put one cube on top of each turtle. Write the number. Move some cubes to the log and the others to the rock. Draw the cubes. Write the numbers. Compare your drawing to others in the class.

244

Name _____

1

5

2

3

4

Directions 1–4 Tell a story about how the picture shows adding one. Write how many in all.

1

_____

- - - - - - - - - - - -

_____

2

_____

- - - - - - - - - - - -

_____

3

_____

- - - - - - - - - - - -

_____

4

_____

- - - - - - - - - - - -

_____

Directions 1–4 Tell a story about how the picture shows adding one. Write how many in all.

At Home Help your child model adding 1 to numbers 0 through 9. For example, use 3 spoons, add one more, and have your child tell how many spoons there are altogether.

Name _____

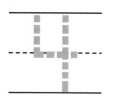

1

◯ ◯ ◯ ◯

2 + 2 = 4

2

5 + 2 = _____

3

1 + 2 = _____

Directions 1–3 Show each number with counters. Draw. Write how many in all.

▲ 1

$$3 \quad + \quad 2 \quad = \quad \underline{\hspace{2cm}}$$

2

$$0 \quad + \quad 2 \quad = \quad \underline{\hspace{2cm}}$$

3

$$4 \quad + \quad 2 \quad = \quad \underline{\hspace{2cm}}$$

Directions 1–3 Show each number with counters.
Draw. Write how many in all.

At Home Let your child use pennies or other small
items to show you how to add 5 and 2, 2 and 2, and 1
and 2. Have your child tell you how many in all.

Name _____

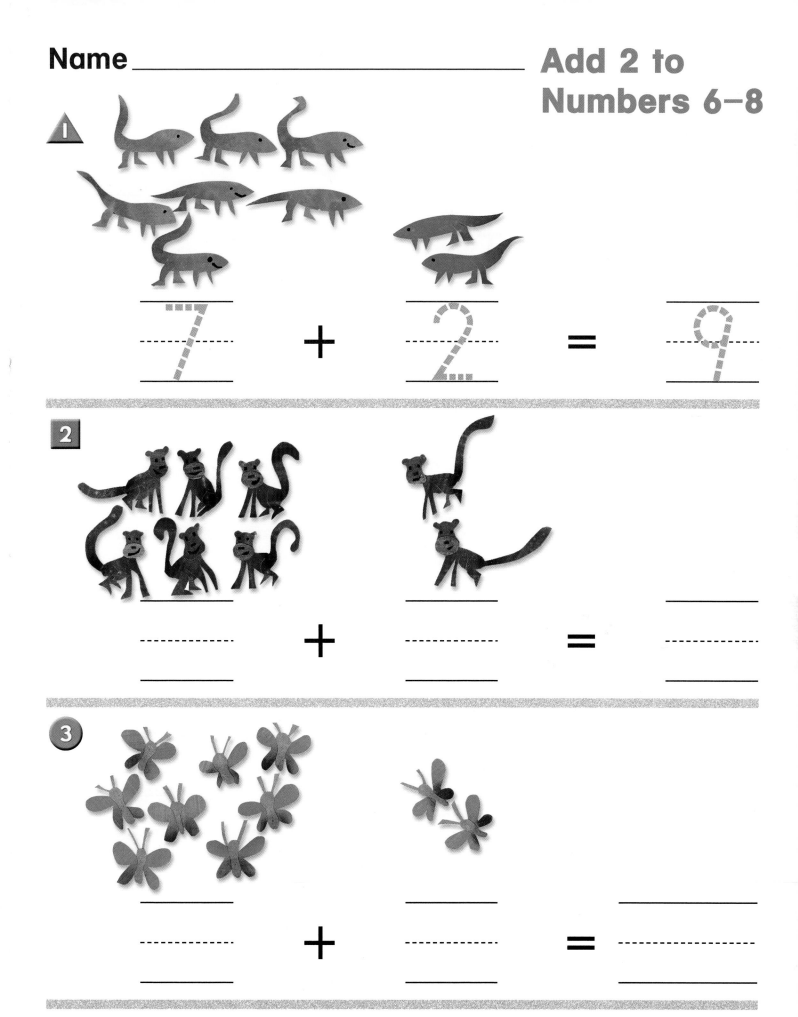

1

$$7 + 2 = 9$$

2

___ + ___ = ___

3

___ + ___ = ___

Directions 1–3 Write the number in each group. Add. Write the sum.

1

_____
. . . .   **+**   . . . .   **=**   . . . .
_____   _____   _____

2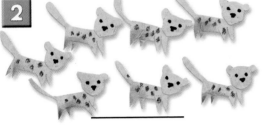

_____   _____   _____
. . . .   **+**   . . . .   **=**   . . . .
_____   _____   _____

3   **Algebra Readiness ▶ Patterns**

_____

1	+	2	=	. . . . _____
2	+	2	=	. . . . _____
3	+	2	=	. . . . _____
_____	+	2	=	. . . . _____

Directions 1–2 Write the number in each group.
Add. Write the sum. **3** Look for a pattern. Complete
each number sentence.

At Home Have your child draw dots or simple
shapes to show adding 8 and 2. Then help your
child record the number sentence 8 + 2 = 10.

Name_____   Add Pennies

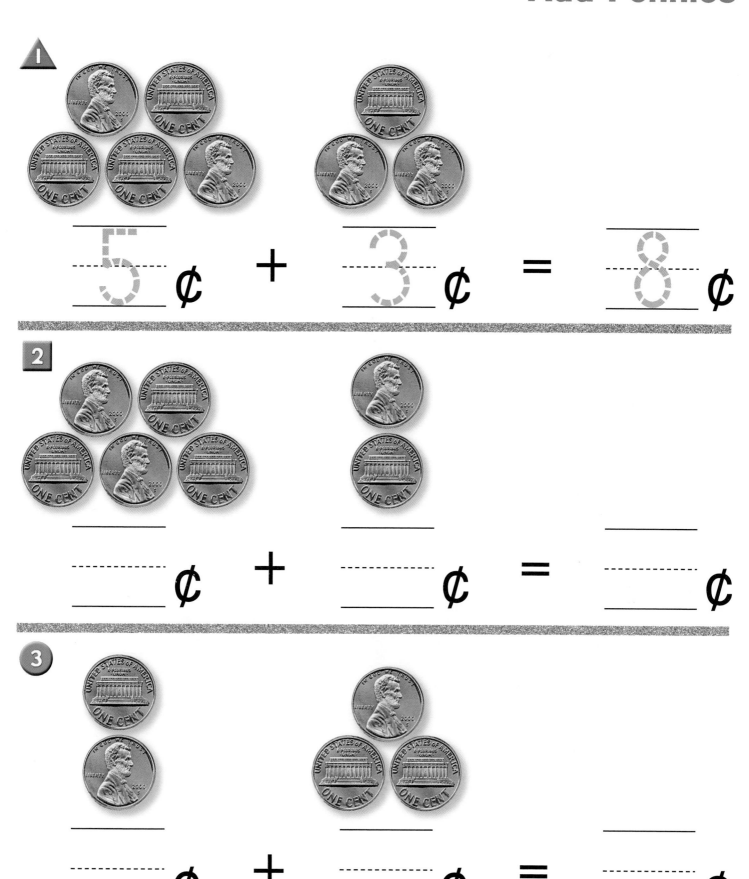

1

$$\underline{5}¢ \quad + \quad \underline{3}¢ \quad = \quad \underline{8}¢$$

2

$$\underline{}¢ \quad + \quad \underline{}¢ \quad = \quad \underline{}¢$$

3

$$\underline{}¢ \quad + \quad \underline{}¢ \quad = \quad \underline{}¢$$

Directions 1–3 Write the number in each group. Add. Write the sum.

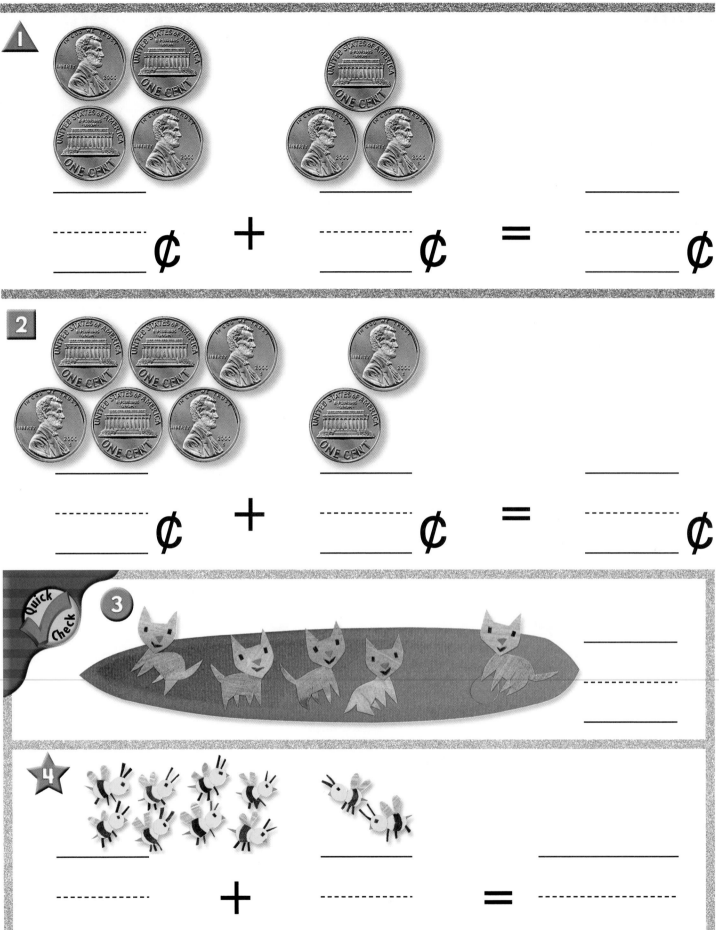

1

_____

_____ ¢ + _____ ¢ = _____ ¢

2

_____

_____ ¢ + _____ ¢ = _____ ¢

3

_____

_____

4

_____ _____ _____

+ =

_____ _____ _____

Directions 1–2 Write the number in each group. Add. Write the sum. **3** Write how many in all. **4** Write the number in each group. Add. Write the sum.

At Home Provide your child with pennies. Have him or her model facts, such as 4 + 3, 7 + 3, and 8 + 2, and tell the sum for each fact.

252

Practice
Addition

△ 1

$$3 + 4 = 7$$

2

$$\underline{} + \underline{} = \underline{}$$

3

$$\underline{} + \underline{} = \underline{}$$

Directions 1–3 Write the number in each group. Add. Write the sum.

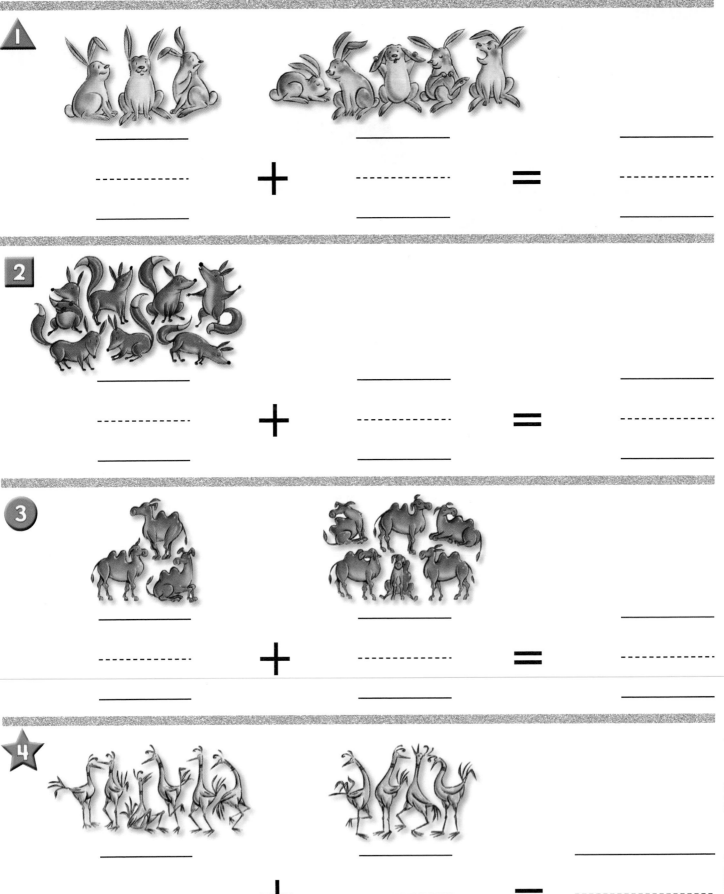

1

_____   +   _____   =   _____

_____   _____   _____

2

_____   +   _____   =   _____

_____   _____   _____

3

_____   +   _____   =   _____

_____   _____   _____

4

_____   +   _____   =   _____

_____   _____   _____

Directions 1–4 Write the number in each group. Add.
Write the sum.

At Home Help your child tell addition stories and
write the accompanying addition sentence. For
example: We have 3 boys and 2 girls in the family.
3 + 2 = 5 people.

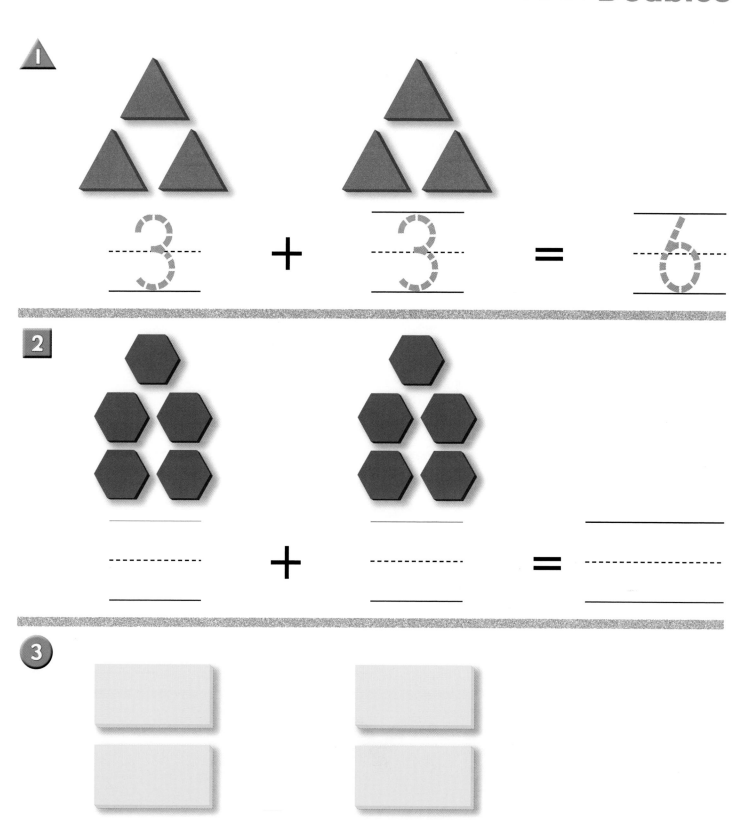

Directions 1–3 Write the number in each group. Add. Write the sum.

1

_____   _____   _____

------------- **+** ------------- **=** -------------

_____   _____   _____

2

_____   _____   _____

------------- **+** ------------- **=** -------------

_____   _____   _____

3

_____   _____   _____

------------- **+** ------------- **=** -------------

_____   _____   _____

4

_____   _____   _____

------------- **+** ------------- **=** -------------

_____   _____   _____

Directions 1–4 Write the number in each group. Add. Write the sum.

At Home Give your child pennies or other small items. Have him or her show you some addition doubles such as 2 + 2 and 5 + 5.

256

Draw a Picture

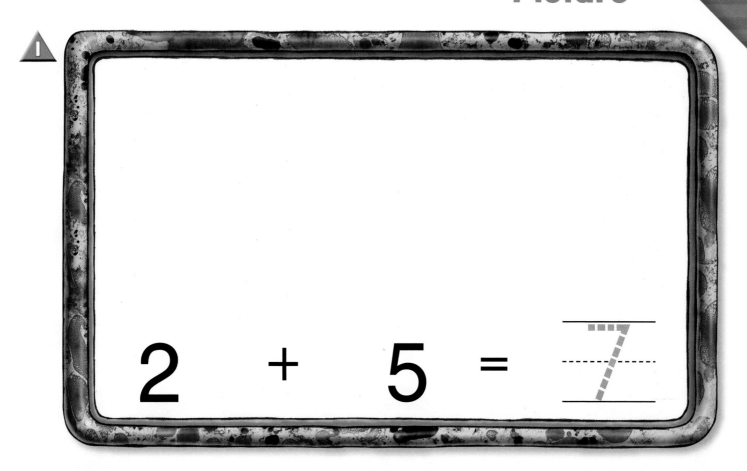

1. 2 + 5 = 7

2. 4 + 4 = ___

Directions 1–2 Draw a picture to match the fact. Add. Write the sum.

$$4 + 5 = \underline{\qquad}$$

$$6 + 1 = \underline{\qquad}$$

Directions 1–2 Draw a picture to match the fact. Add. Write the sum.

At Home Have your child tell stories about the pictures he or she has drawn. Have your child explain how he or she found the answer.

Feeding Time at the ZOO

This take-home book will help you review concepts you learned in Chapter 13.

1

Tony feeds the monkeys.

How many monkeys are eating?

_____   _____   _____

_____ + _____ = _____

3

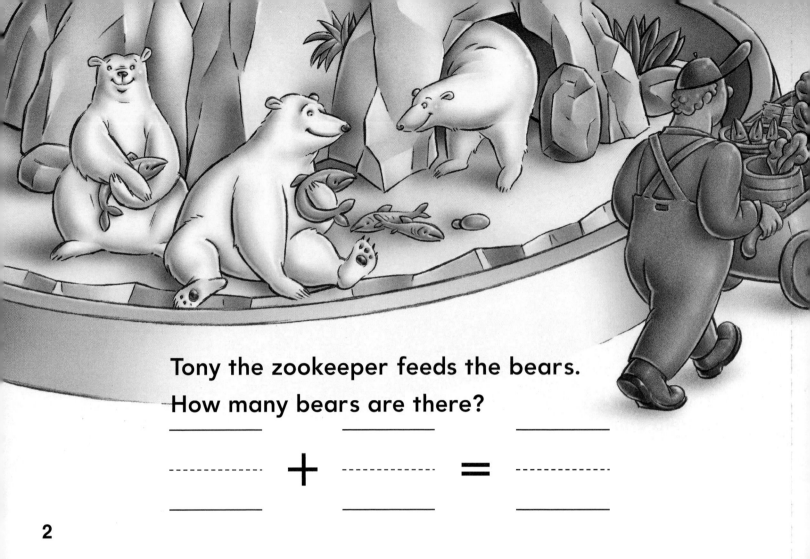

Tony the zookeeper feeds the bears.
How many bears are there?

_____   _____   _____
------------ **+** ------------ **=** ------------
_____   _____   _____

2

Tony feeds the zebras.
How many zebras does Tony feed?

_____   _____   _____
------------ **+** ------------ **=** ------------
_____   _____   _____

4

Tony feeds the seals.

How many seals are there?

_____   _____   _____

$+$ - - - - - - - - $=$ - - - - - - - -

_____   _____   _____

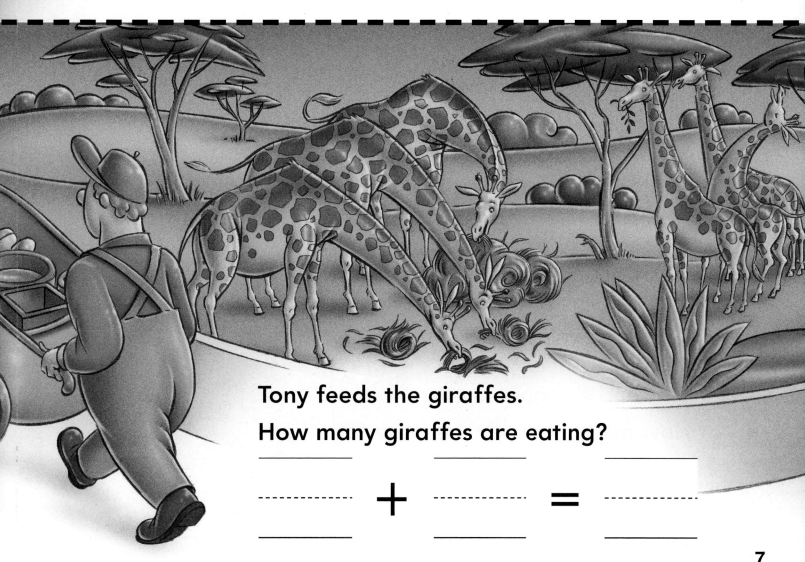

Tony feeds the giraffes.

How many giraffes are eating?

_____   _____   _____

$+$ - - - - - - - - $=$ - - - - - - - -

_____   _____   _____

Tony feeds the birds.

How many birds are there?

_____   _____   _____

_ _ _ _ _ _ _ _ + _ _ _ _ _ _ _ = _ _ _ _ _ _ _

_____   _____   _____

6

We feed the goats.

How many cents do we have together?

_____   _____   _____

_ _ _ _ _ _ ¢ + _ _ _ _ _ _ ¢ = _ _ _ _ _ _ ¢

8

Name _____

1

——————

- - - - - - - -

——————

2

——————   ——————   ——————

- - - - - - - -   **+**   - - - - - - - -   **=**   - - - - - - - -

——————   ——————   ——————

3

——————   ——————   ——————

- - - - - - - - ¢   **+**   - - - - - - - - ¢   **=**   - - - - - - - - ¢

——————   ——————   ——————

4

——————

$$6 \quad + \quad 3 \quad =$$ - - - - - - - -

——————

Directions 1 Write how many in all. **2–3** Write the number in each group. Add. Write the sum.
4 Draw a picture to match the fact. Add. Write the sum.

Chapter 13

259

Art Connection

1

_____   _____   _____

----------- **+** ----------- **=** -----------

_____   _____   _____

2

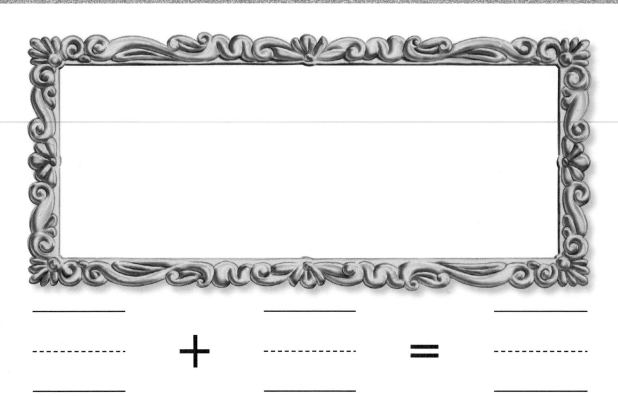

_____   _____   _____

----------- **+** ----------- **=** -----------

_____   _____   _____

Directions 1 Tell an addition story about the animals in the picture. Write the addition sentence. **2** Draw your own picture. Tell an addition story. Write the addition sentence.

Practice
Subtraction

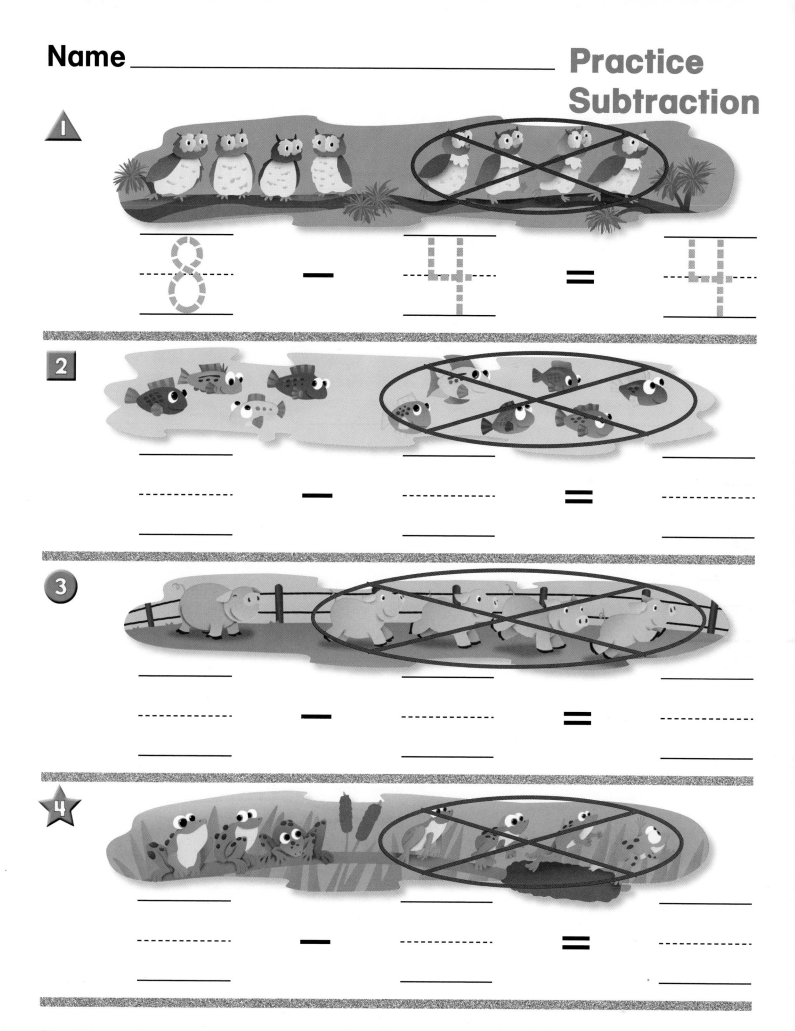

1.   8   −   4   =   4

2.   ___   −   ___   =   ___

3.   ___   −   ___   =   ___

4.   ___   −   ___   =   ___

Directions 1–4 Write a subtraction sentence to match the picture.

1

_____   _____   _____

------------ ▬ ------------ ═ ------------

_____   _____   _____

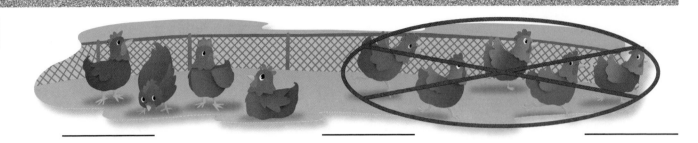

2

_____   _____   _____

------------ ▬ ------------ ═ ------------

_____   _____   _____

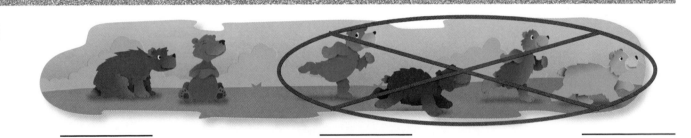

3

_____   _____   _____

------------ ▬ ------------ ═ ------------

_____   _____   _____

_____   _____   _____

------------ ▬ ------------ ═ ------------

_____   _____   _____

Directions 1–4 Write a subtraction sentence to match the picture.

At Home Help your child tell subtraction stories and write the accompanying subtraction sentence. For example: 6 people were sitting at the table. 2 went to the other room. 6 − 2 = 4 people still at the table.

Choose the Operation

1

2 3 = ‾5‾

2

7 3 = _____

3

5 ◯ 4 = _____

Directions 1–3 Tell a story to match the picture. Decide if it shows addition or subtraction.
Write a plus or minus sign in the circle. Write the answer.

1

6 ◯ 4 = _____

2

4 ◯ 6 = _____

3

9 ◯ 3 = _____

Directions 1–3 Tell a story to match the picture. Decide if it shows addition or subtraction. Write a plus or minus sign in the circle. Write the answer.

At Home Have your child tell you how he or she knew whether to add or subtract for each picture.

AWAY THEY GO!

This take-home book will help you review concepts you learned in Chapter 14.

1

One baby bunny hops away.
How many bunnies stay to play?

$$\boxed{} - \boxed{} = \boxed{}$$

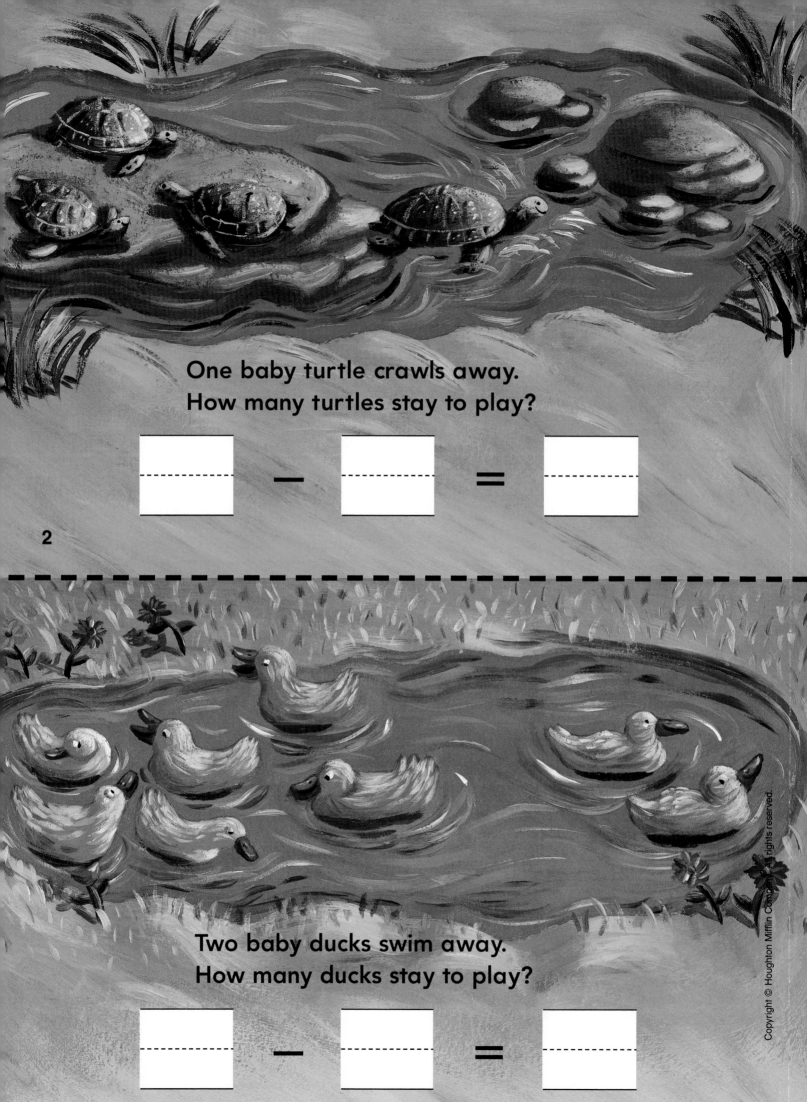

One baby turtle crawls away.
How many turtles stay to play?

$$\boxed{} - \boxed{} = \boxed{}$$

2

Two baby ducks swim away.
How many ducks stay to play?

$$\boxed{} - \boxed{} = \boxed{}$$

4

Two baby birds fly away.
How many birds stay to play?

☐ − ☐ = ☐

5

Three baby skunks walk away.
How many skunks stay to play?

☐ − ☐ = ☐

7

Two baby deer run away.
How many deer stay to play?

☐ − ☐ = ☐

6

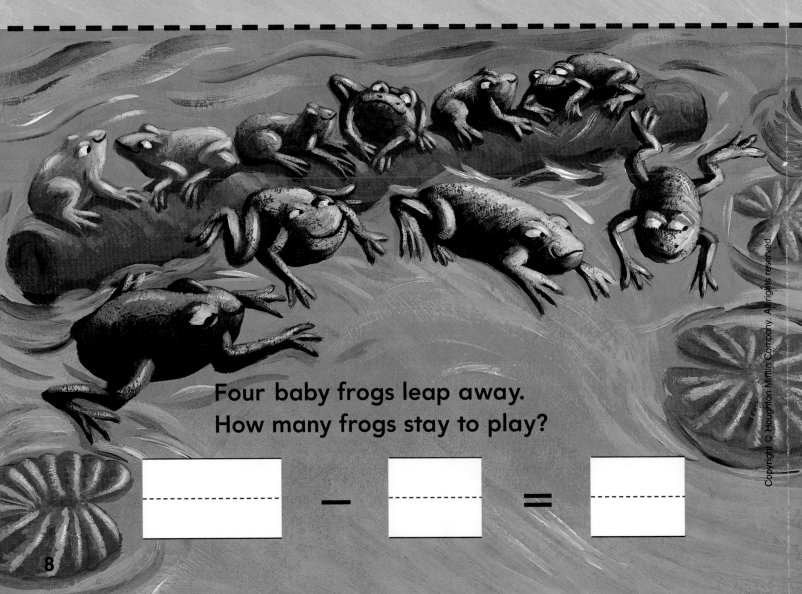

Four baby frogs leap away.
How many frogs stay to play?

☐ − ☐ = ☐

8

Name _____

1

_____

_____

2

$$7 - 2 = $$

_____

_____

3

_____ ¢ − _____ ¢ = _____ ¢

4

$$6 \bigcirc 3 = $$

_____

_____

Directions 1 Circle and cross out the one that is leaving. Write how many are left. 2 Draw balls to show the first number. Circle and cross out a group of two. Write how many are left. 3 Write a subtraction sentence to match the picture. 4 Decide if the picture shows addition or subtraction. Write a plus or minus sign in the circle. Write the answer.

Add or Subtract 1

What You Need

How to Play **1** Take turns with a partner. **2** Roll the number cube and move that number of spaces. **3** Count the dots. Add or subtract 1. Tell your number sentence. **4** Play until a player reaches Finish.

Name _____

_____

- - - - - - -

_____

2

_____   _____   _____

- - - - - - **+** - - - - - - **=** - - - - - -

_____   _____   _____

3

_____   _____   _____

- - - - - - **+** - - - - - - **=** - - - - - -

_____ **¢**   _____ **¢**   _____ **¢**

$$5 \quad + \quad 4 \quad = \quad$$

_____

- - - - - -

_____

Directions 1 Write how many in all. **2–3** Write the number in each group. Add. Write the sum.
4 Draw a picture to match the fact. Add. Write the sum.

5

_____

- - - - - - -

_____

6

$$5 \quad - \quad 2 \quad =$$

_____

- - - - - - -

_____

7

_____ ¢   −   _____ ¢   =   _____ ¢

8

$$4 \quad \bigcirc \quad 2 \quad =$$

_____

- - - - - - -

_____

Directions **5** Circle and cross out the one that is leaving. Write how many are left. **6** Draw balls to show the first number. Circle and cross out a group of two. Write how many are left. **7** Write a subtraction sentence to match the pennies. **8** Decide if the picture shows addition or subtraction. Write a plus or minus sign in the circle. Write the answer.

278

Name _____

Missing Addends

1

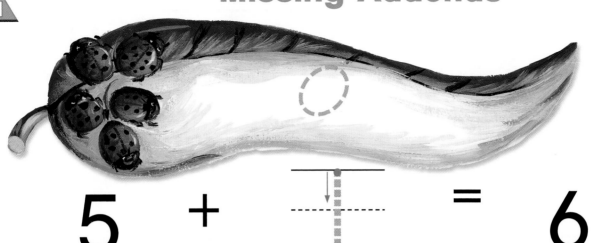

$$5 + \underline{\quad} = 6$$

2

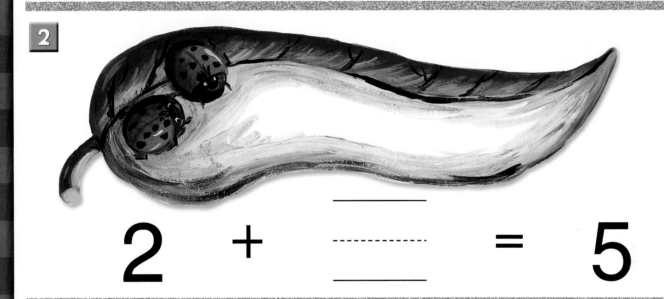

$$2 + \underline{\quad} = 5$$

3

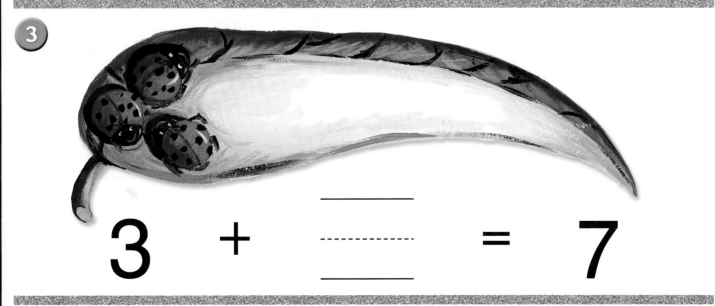

$$3 + \underline{\quad} = 7$$

Directions 1–3 Count the ladybugs. Draw more to make the sum. Write the missing number to complete the number sentence.

WEEKLY WR READER® Activity Almanac

See page 330.

Cumulative Review

1

_____
- - - - - - - - - - - - - - :00
_____

2

_____
- - - - - - - - - - - - - -
_____ ¢

3

_____   _____   _____
- - - - - -   **+**   - - - - - -   **=**   - - - - - -
_____   _____   _____

4

5

Directions 1 Write the time shown. 2 Write the number of cents. 3 Write the number in each group. Add. Write the sum. 4 Circle the heavier one. Underline the lighter one. 5 Circle the fourth one. Underline the second one.

Photography Credits: 260 © Ascott House, Buckinghamshire, UK/Bridgeman Art Library. **Illustration Credits:** 242–244, 249–250, 252, 256 © Bob Barner. 245–246, 253–254, 257–260, Chapter 13 Story © Tracy Sabin. 261–262, Chapter 14 Story, 276, 279 © Diane Greenseid. 263–264, 267–268, 270–275, 277–278, 280(b) © Robin Boyer. 280(tl) © Mark and Rosemary Jarman.

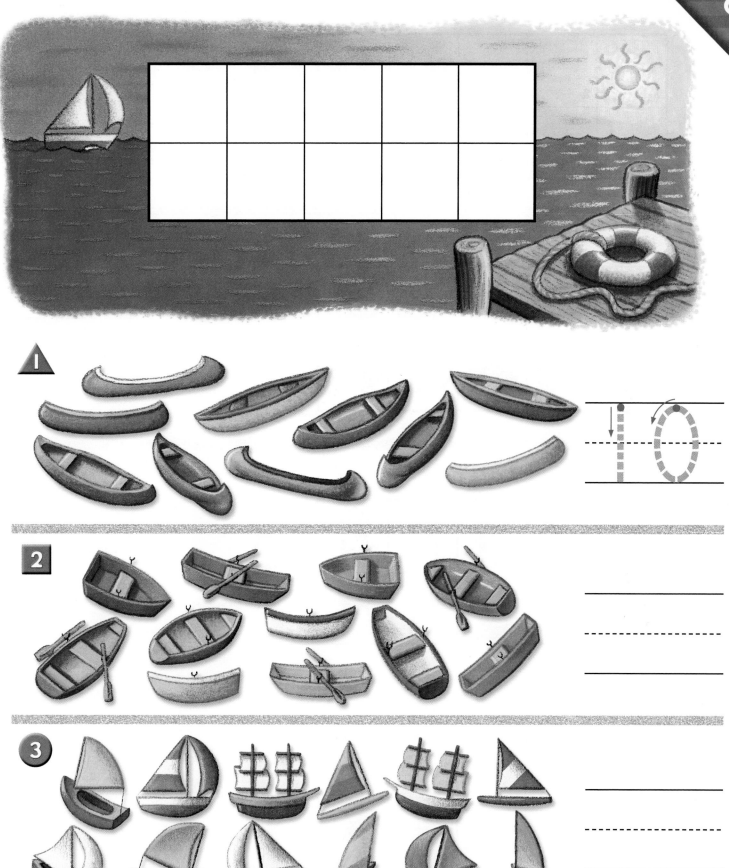

1

2

3

Directions 1–3 Place a counter on each item. Move the counters to the ten-frame.
Count the filled ten-frame as 10 and then count the extras. Write the number.

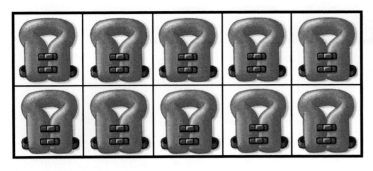 

_____
- - - - - - - - - - - - - - - -
_____

2

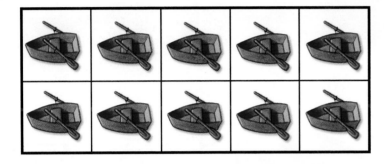

_____
- - - - - - - - - - - - - - - -
_____

3

_____
- - - - - - - - - - - - - - - -
_____

★ **4**

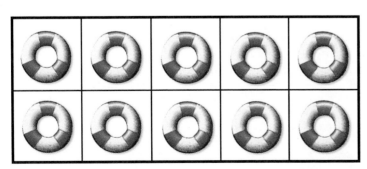

_____
- - - - - - - - - - - - - - - -
_____

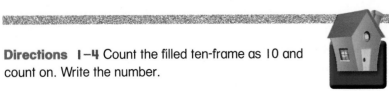

Directions 1–4 Count the filled ten-frame as 10 and count on. Write the number.

At Home Let your child count groups of 10, 11, and 12 small objects and practice writing each number.

Name _____ Numbers 19–20

  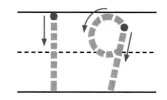

2

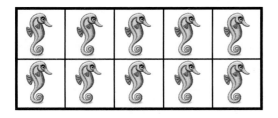 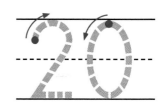

3

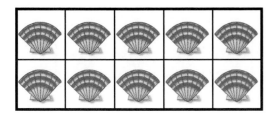 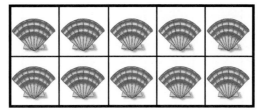

⭐

Directions 1–4 Count the filled ten-frames by tens and count on. Write the number.

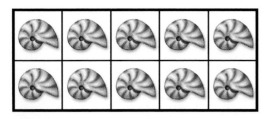

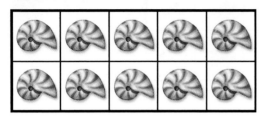

18   19   (20)

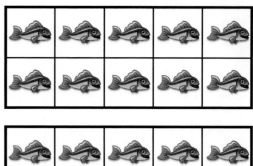

18   19   20

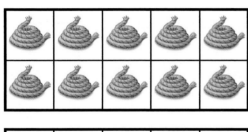

18   19   20

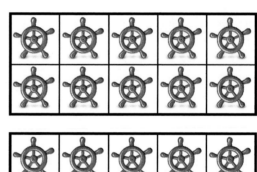

18   19   20

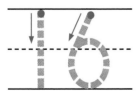 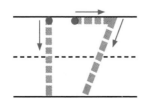 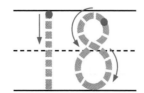 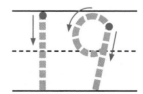 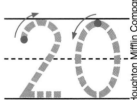

Directions 1–4 Count the items. Circle the number.
5 Write each number.

At Home Have your child count out 20 small objects, such as paper clips, and show you that 20 is two groups of 10.

294

Order Numbers 10–20

Directions Count the filled ten-frame as 10 and count on. Write each number.

10 11 12 13 14 15 16 17 18 19 20

10 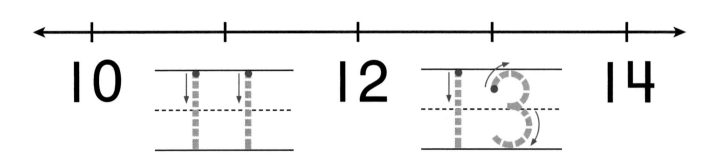 12 13 14

2

13 _____ 15 _____ 17

3

16 _____ 18 _____ 20

Directions 1–3 Write the missing numbers.

At Home Write the numbers 10 through 20 on small pieces of paper and mix them up. Have your child put the pieces in order and then point to and say each number.

Copyright © Houghton Mifflin Company. All rights reserved.

296

Name _____

                    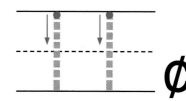

¢

2

_____

- - - - - - - - - - - - - - - - -

_____ ¢

3

_____

- - - - - - - - - - - - - - - - -

_____ ¢

_____

- - - - - - - - - - - - - - - - -

_____ ¢

Directions 1–4 Point to the dime and say "ten cents." Point to each penny as you count on to find the number of cents in all. Write the number of cents.

1

_____

- - - - - - - - - - - - - - - - - -

_____ ¢

2

_____

- - - - - - - - - - - - - - - - - -

_____ ¢

3

_____

- - - - - - - - - - - - - - - - - -

_____ ¢

4

_____

- - - - - - - - - - - - - - - - - -

_____ ¢

5

_____

- - - - - - - - - - - - - - - - - -

_____ ¢

Directions 1–5 Point to the dime and say "ten cents." Point to each penny as you count on to find the number of cents in all. Write the number of cents.

At Home Let your child use one dime and nine pennies to show you amounts of money from 10¢ through 19¢.

298

Name_____

Guess   Check

more than 10
less than 10
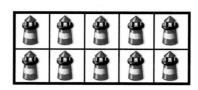
_ _ _ _ _ _ _ _ _ _ _ _

2

Guess   Check

more than 10
less than 10

_ _ _ _ _ _ _ _ _ _ _ _

3

Guess   Check

more than 10
less than 10

_ _ _ _ _ _ _ _ _ _ _ _

Guess   Check

more than 10
less than 10
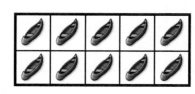
_ _ _ _ _ _ _ _ _ _ _ _

Directions 1–4 Guess whether the picture shows less than 10 or more than 10. Circle your guess. Count to check your answer. Write the number.

Chapter 15   **299**

Guess

Check

more than 15
less than 15

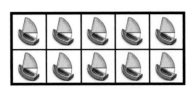 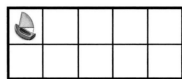

2

Guess

Check

more than 15
less than 15

3

Guess

Check

more than 15
less than 15

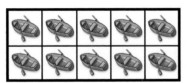 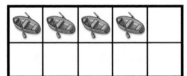

Guess

Check

more than 15
less than 15

Directions 1–4 Guess whether the picture shows less than 15 or more than 15. Circle your guess. Count to check your answer. Write the number.

At Home Have your child explain how he or she made each estimate (guess). Then have your child explain how the numbers match the pictures.

300

Counting Sea Treasures

This take-home book will help you review concepts you learned in Chapter 15.

1

Some shells are rough.

How many are rough?

3

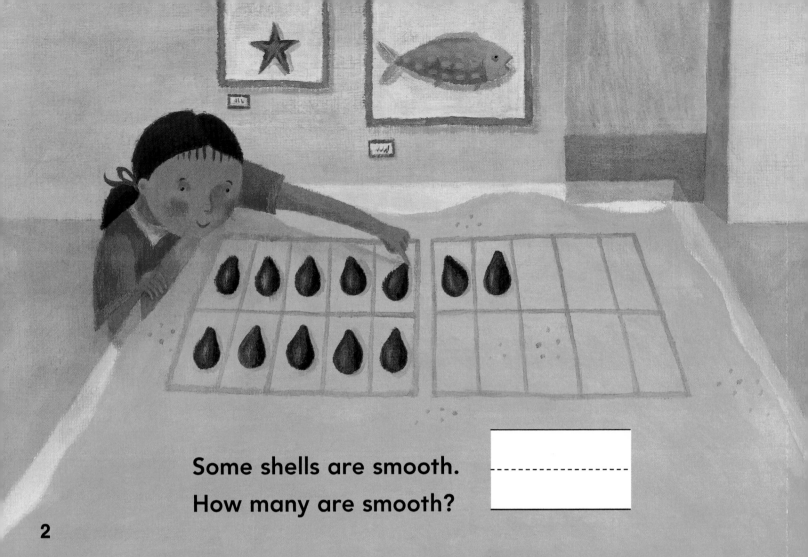

Some shells are smooth.
How many are smooth?

2

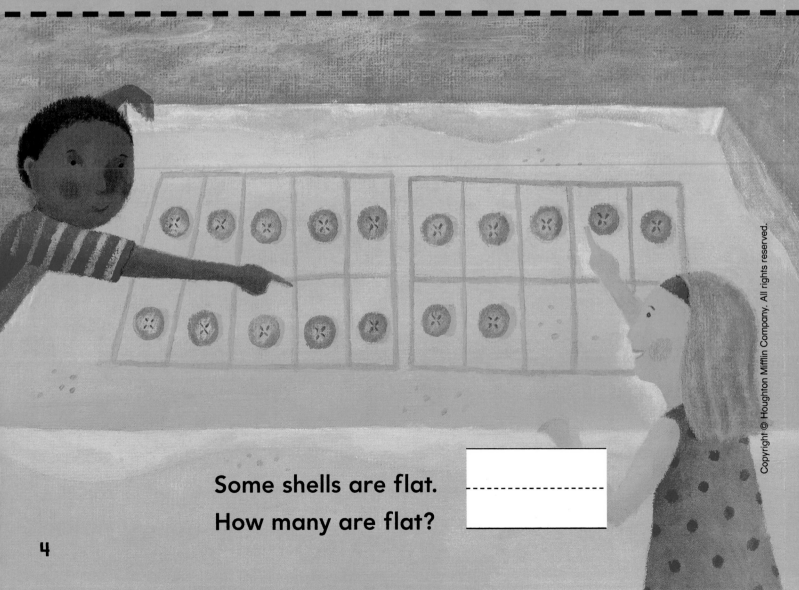

Some shells are flat.
How many are flat?

4

Some shells are round.
How many are round?

5

Sea horses are curvy.
How many are curvy?

7

Sea stars are pointy.
How many are pointy?

6

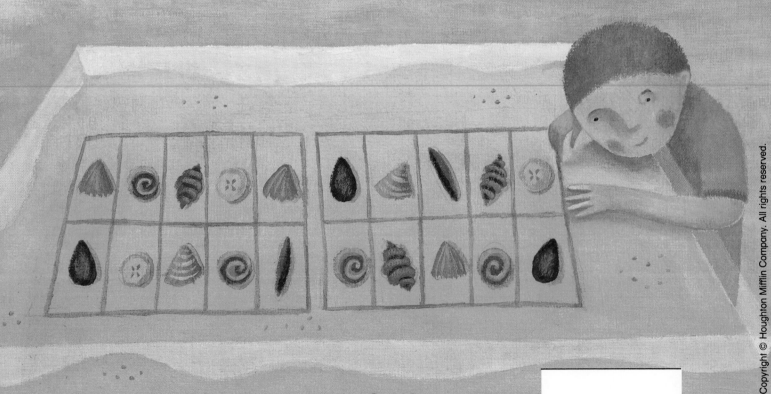

Shells come in lots of colors, too!
How many shells do you see?

8

Name _____

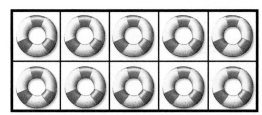 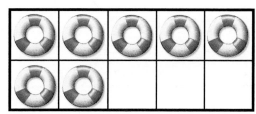

_____
- - - - - - - - - - - -
_____

2

15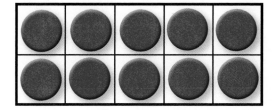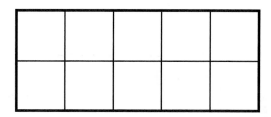

3

15 ____ 17 ____ 19
- - - - - - - - - - - -
_____   - - - - - - - - - - - -
_____

Guess   Check
                                         _____
more than 10   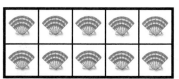 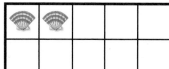   - - - - - - - - - -
less than 10   _____

Directions 1 Count. Write the number. 2 Count. Draw more circles to make the number shown. 3 Write the missing numbers. 4 Guess whether the picture shows more or less than 10. Circle your guess. Count to check your answer. Write the number.

Chapter 15   301

1

2

3

more than 20 ☆   less than 20 ☆

Directions Talk about the Fourth of July celebration. **1** Count the number of flags. Write the number.
2 Count the number of stripes on a flag. Write the number. **3** Guess whether there are less than 20 or
more than 20 stars on the large flag. Count to check. Circle the answer.

Calendar: Using Numbers 1–31

July

Sunday	Monday	Tuesday	Wednesday	Thursday	Friday	Saturday
			1	2	3	4
5	6	7	8	9	10	11
12	13	14	15	16	17	18
19	20	21	22	23	24	25
26	27	28	29	30	31	

Directions Follow the teacher's directions to circle the dates.

Sunday	Monday	Tuesday	Wednesday	Thursday	Friday	Saturday

Directions Make a calendar for the current month. Write the name of the month and the dates.

At Home Have your child point to the days of the week and the dates of all the Saturdays. Then have your child read several dates to you.

310

Name ______________________________

Count by Twos, Fives, Tens

1

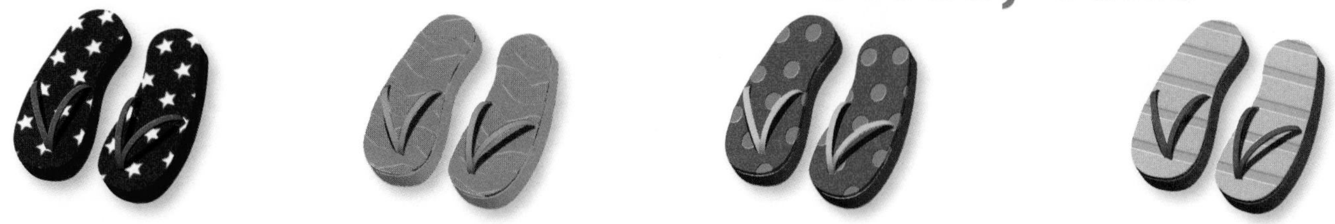

2 4 ___ ___

10 ___ ___ ___

2

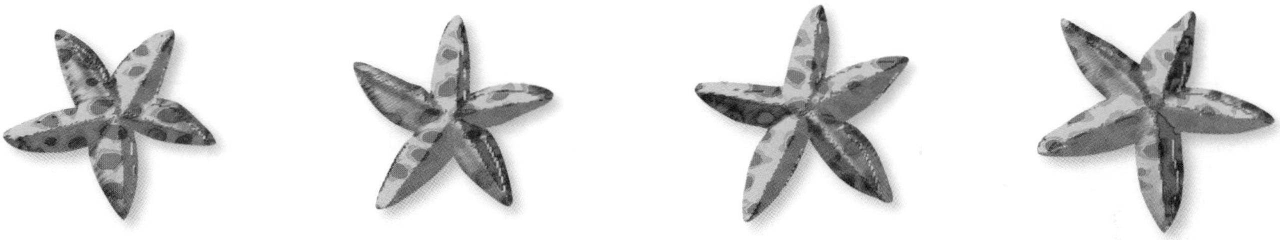

5 10 ___ ___

3

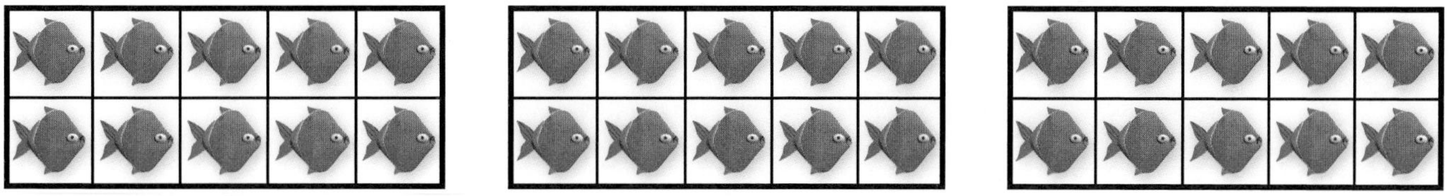

10 ___ ___

Directions 1 Count by twos. Write the numbers. 2 Count by fives. Write the numbers. 3 Count by tens. Write the numbers.

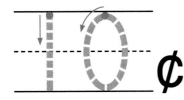 $\cancel{c}$ _____ $\cancel{c}$ _____ $\cancel{c}$

 $\cancel{c}$ _____ $\cancel{c}$ _____ $\cancel{c}$ _____ $\cancel{c}$

3

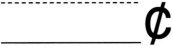 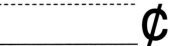

_____

- - - - - - -

⭐ **4**

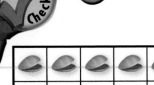

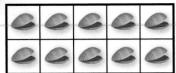

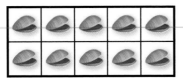

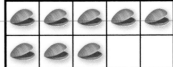

_____

- - - - - - -

_____

Directions 1 Count by tens. Write the cents. 2 Count by fives. Write the cents. 3–4 Count by tens and then count on. Write the number.

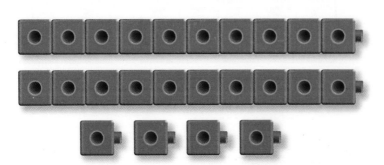

At Home Encourage your child to count aloud by twos, fives, and tens.

312

Use a Pattern

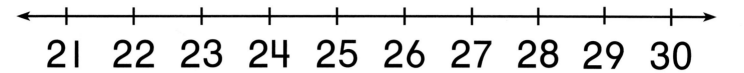

21 22 23 24 25 26 27 28 29 30

1

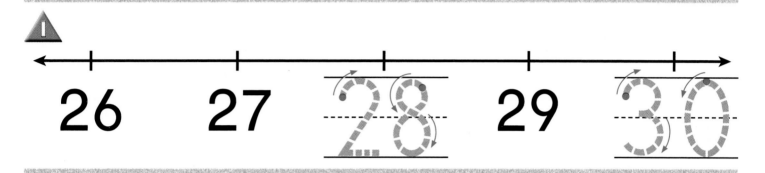

26   27   *28*   29   *30*

2

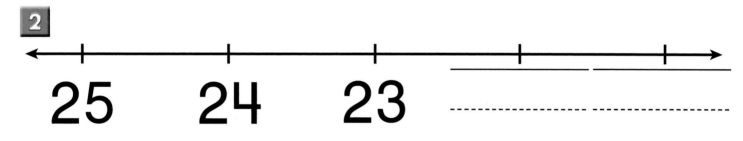

25   24   23   ___   ___

3

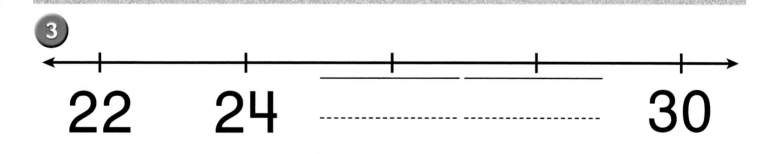

22   24   ___   ___   30

4

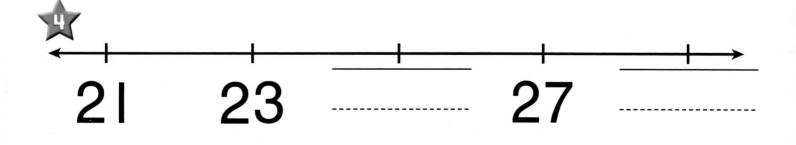

21   23   ___   27   ___

Directions 1–4 Look for a pattern. Write the missing numbers.
Use the number line to help.

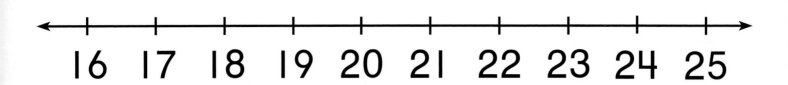

16 17 18 19 20 21 22 23 24 25

△ 1

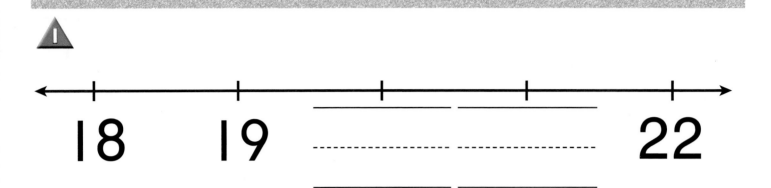

18   19   _____ _____   22

2

18   19   18   _____ _____

3

16 _____   20 _____   24

★ 4

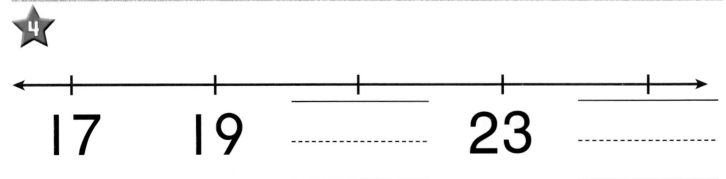

17   19   _____   23   _____

Directions 1–4 Look for a pattern. Write the missing numbers. Use the number line to help.

At Home Let your child explain several of the patterns and how he or she decided what the missing numbers were.

314

BEAR'S BEACH PARTY

I invited lots of friends.   ------------------

How many are coming?   _____

1

3

I am having a beach party today!
What is the date?

_____

_____

2

Dad blows up beach balls.
How many do you see?

_____

_____

4

Mom pours some drinks. ----------------------

How many cups do you see? _____

Grandpa hands out hats. ----------------------

How many do you see? _____

Grandma makes some snacks. --------------------

How many do you see? _____

6

Everyone gets a balloon! --------------------

Count the balloons by twos, fives, or tens. _____

8

Name _____

23   24   25

27   28   29

25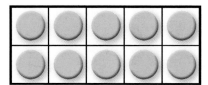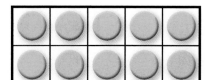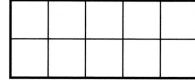

_____   _____

_____   28   29   _____   31

_____   _____

25   24   _____   _____   21

Directions 1−2 Count the cube trains by tens and then count on. Circle the number. 3 Count.
Draw more dots to make the number shown. 4 Write the missing numbers. 5 Look for a pattern.
Write the missing numbers.

Swim to 31

Practice GAME

What You Need

How to Play 1 Take turns with a partner. 2 Roll the number cube and move that number of spaces. 3 Read the number on the space. If you land on 10, 20, or 30, roll again. 4 Play until a player reaches or passes 31.

Name_____

14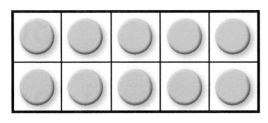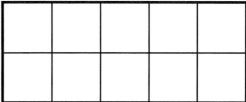

_____

- - - - - - - - - -

2

 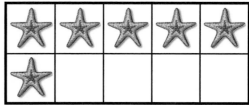

_____

- - - - - - - - - -

3

13   14   _____   16   _____

- - - - - - - -   - - - - - - -

_____   _____

4

Guess   Check

                                                    _____

more than 15      - - - - - - -

less than 15   _____

Directions 1 Count. Draw more dots to make the number shown. Write the number. **2** Count.
Write the number. **3** Write the missing numbers. **4** Circle your guess. Count to check your answer.
Write the number.

5

28

29

30

6

20

25

30

7

28

8

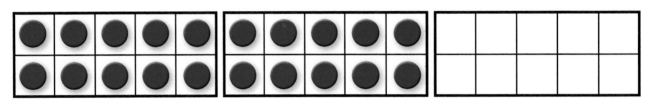

21 22 _____ 24 _____ 26

9

20 22 _____ _____ 28

Directions 5–6 Count the cube trains by tens and then count on. Circle the number. **7** Count.
Draw more dots to make the number shown. **8** Write the missing numbers. **9** Look for a pattern.
Write the missing numbers.

Hundred Chart

1	2	3	4	5	6	7	8	9	10
11	12	13	14	15	16	17	18	19	20
21	22	23	24	25	26	27	28	29	30
31	32	33	34	35	36	37	38	39	40
41	42	43	44	45	46	47	48	49	50
51	52	53	54	55	56	57	58	59	60
61	62	63	64	65	66	67	68	69	70
71	72	73	74	75	76	77	78	79	80
81	82	83	84	85	86	87	88	89	90
91	92	93	94	95	96	97	98	99	100

Directions 1 Color in yellow all the numbers in the last column. Count by tens. **2** Put a blue X on all the numbers that end with a 5 or 0. Count by fives. **3** Circle in red every other number starting with 2. Count by twos.

WEEKLY WR **READER® Activity Almanac**

See page 331.

Name _____

Cumulative Review

 1

2

3

‾‾‾‾‾‾‾   ‾‾‾‾‾‾‾   ‾‾‾‾‾‾‾

 **+** **=**

‾‾‾‾‾‾‾   ‾‾‾‾‾‾‾   ‾‾‾‾‾‾‾

4

‾‾‾‾‾‾‾   ‾‾‾‾‾‾‾   ‾‾‾‾‾‾‾

- **−** - **=** -

‾‾‾‾‾‾‾   ‾‾‾‾‾‾‾   ‾‾‾‾‾‾‾

5

‾‾‾‾‾‾‾   ‾‾‾‾‾‾‾   ‾‾‾‾‾‾‾

18 19 _____ _____ 22 _____

Directions 1 Circle the one that shows equal parts. 2 Circle the one that holds more. Underline the one that holds less. 3 Write the number in each group. Add. Write the sum. 4 Write a subtraction sentence to match the picture. 5 Write the missing numbers.

Photography Credits: 290(t), 290(tm), 292(t), 292(bl), 292(br) © C Squared Studios/PhotoDisc/Getty Images. 290(b), 292(m) © Stockbyte/PictureQuest. 291(b) © Ken Karp. **Illustration Credits:** 282(tr), 283–284, Chapter 15 Story, 302 © Katherine Lucas. 282(bl), 285–288, 293–294, 299–301 © Erika LeBarre. 303–304, 307–312, 316–317, 320 © Lyn Boyer. Chapter 16 Story © Rose Mary Berlin.

1 2 3 4 5 6 7 8 9 – WC – 12 11 10 09 08 07 06 05 04 03

Strand: Number and Operations

Competency Goal 1: The learner will recognize, model, and write whole numbers through 30.

Objectives	Houghton Mifflin Math
1.01 Develop number sense for whole numbers through 30. • Connect model, number word (orally), and number, using a variety of representations. • Count objects in a set. • Read and write numerals. • Compare and order sets and numbers. • Use ordinals (1st–10th). • Estimate quantities fewer than or equal to 10. • Recognize equivalence in sets and numbers 1–10.	Ch. 3, pp. 45–50; Ch. 4, pp. 59–70, 73, 74; Ch. 7, pp. 125–134, 137–140; Ch. 8, pp. 145–148, 151, 152; Ch. 9, pp. 169, 170; Ch. 10, pp. 185–190, 193, 194; Ch. 13, pp. 245–256; Ch. 15, pp. 285–298; Ch. 16, pp. 305–314
1.02 Share equally (divide) between two people; explain.	Ch. 5, pp. 97, 98
1.03 Solve problems and share solutions to problems in small groups.	Whole/Small group activities in class

Strand: Measurement

Competency Goal 2: The learner will explore concepts of measurement

Objectives	Houghton Mifflin Math
2.01 Compare attributes of two objects using appropriate vocabulary (color, weight, height, width, length, texture).	Ch. 1, pp. 5–16; Ch. 11, pp. 205, 206; Ch. 12, pp. 219, 220
2.02 Recognize concepts of calendar time using appropriate vocabulary (days of the week, months of the year, seasons).	Ch. 9, pp. 167–170; Ch. 16, pp. 309, 310

Strand: Geometry

Competency Goal 3: The learner will explore concepts in geometry.

Objectives	Houghton Mifflin Math
3.01 Identify, build, draw, and name triangles, rectangles, and circles; identify, build, and name spheres and cubes.	Ch. 5, pp. 85–88; Ch. 6, pp. 105–110
3.02 Compare geometric shapes (identify likenesses and differences).	Ch. 5, pp. 85–88; Ch. 6, pp. 105–110
3.03 Model and use directional and positional vocabulary.	Ch. 2, pp. 23–28
3.04 Complete simple spatial visualization tasks and puzzles.	Ch. 6, p. 104; Unit 3, p. 119

Strand: Data Analysis and Probability

Competency Goal 4: The learner will collect, organize and display data

Objectives	Houghton Mifflin Math
4.01 Collect and organize data as a group activity.	Ch. 3, pp. 53, 54
4.02 Display and describe data with concrete and pictorial graphs as a group activity.	Ch. 3, pp. 51–54

Strand: Algebra

Competency Goal 5: The learner will model simple patterns and sort objects.

Objectives	Houghton Mifflin Math
5.01 Sort and classify objects by one attribute.	Ch. 1, pp. 5–18; Ch. 4, pp. 71, 72; Ch. 8, pp. 149, 150; Ch. 10, pp. 191, 192
5.02 Create and extend patterns with actions, words, and objects.	Ch. 2, pp. 29–34; Ch. 5, pp. 89, 90; Whole/Small group activities in class

Workmat 1

Multi-Purpose Mat

Two-Part Mat

Graphing Grid

Double Ten-Frame

Workmat 6

Whole

Part

Part

Number Lines

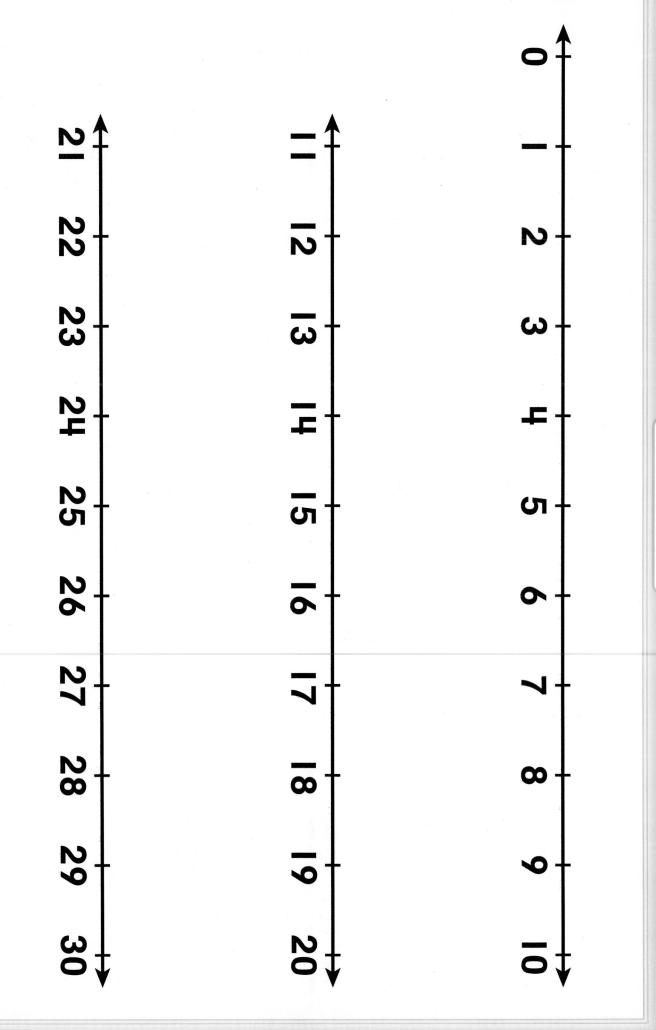

0 1 2 3 4 5 6 7 8 9 10

11 12 13 14 15 16 17 18 19 20

21 22 23 24 25 26 27 28 29 30